Victorious Transformation

STEP INTO THE NEXT BEST YOU

COMPLIED BY

Dr. Pamela Henkel

Published By: DNP Presents

Library of Congress Cataloging-in-Publication Data has been applied for

ISBN: 979-8-9988576-7-6

PRINTED IN THE UNITED STATES OF AMERICA

DEDICATION

To Jesus Christ, the Lover of my soul, my Best Friend, and my King.

The One who brings beauty from ashes, victory from battles, and transformation from surrender.

This book is for Your glory alone. Every story within these pages is a testimony to Your faithfulness, mercy, and unfailing love.

To my precious children — Your lives to me are a continuous legacy of God's promises fulfilled.

Through every season, especially during the difficult times, we have persevered together with faith and determination.

Together, we have witnessed that God is our ever-present Hope and Help, our steady anchor when the winds of challenge blow strong.

You are my pearls and a daily reminder that God's plans are always good and His promises never fail. ♥

And to every author who said "yes" to sharing your heart. Thank you for your story, courage, authenticity, and your obedience to Answer God's Call.

Your voices made this book a symphony of hope, and together we declare that **Victorious Transformation** is not only possible — it is already HERE.

May every word in these pages be an instrument of healing.

May every testimony minister Grace and peace to souls that need it.

May every reader be strengthened, awakened, and propelled into their own **Victorious Transformation** by the power of our Precious Holy Spirit.

And may Jesus Christ — the Author and Finisher of our faith — be glorified in every life this book touches.
In Jesus' Name, Amen

BLESSINGS & Love,

Dr. Pamela

SPECIAL ACKNOWLEDGMENTS

A heartfelt thank you to Dr. Trunnis Goggins—thank you for seeing my dream and choosing to help bring it to life. As a literary agent, I truly could not have asked for more. You believed in me before I fully saw the scope of what God was doing. Your commitment to finding the best way to communicate my heart and story has been both humbling and empowering. Thank you for recognizing the value in my journey, for treating my story as one that needed to be seen and heard, and for seeing a bigger picture of who I was becoming. Your support of this book, of every author within its pages, and your beautiful contribution in writing the foreword—have meant the world.

Dr. Nichol Perricci, thank you for being the wind beneath my wings—especially when moving forward was difficult. You refused to let life's disruptions stall me and reminded me who I am and why this book matters. You are not only an incredible publisher, graphic artist, and business partner—you are a cherished friend. It is an honor to do life and ministry with you. Thank you for standing with me in this process, and for believing in what Victorious Transformation could become.

"The Lord gave the word; great was the company of those who proclaimed it." —Psalm 68:11 (NKJV)

Together, we have declared His goodness—and the ripple effect has only begun.

BLESSINGS,

Dr. Pamela

NOTE FROM THE VISIONARY

Welcome to Victorious Transformation

I have always believed that when we share what God has done in our lives, we don't just tell a story —We build a bridge for someone else's breakthrough.

Victorious Transformation **was birthed by God.** A stirring from the Holy Spirit to gather testimonies that would boldly declare the goodness of God, the power of His Word and the beauty of His redeeming love.

Every chapter is a reminder that no matter how deep the valley or fierce the storm, God's plan is always greater, His grace always sufficient, and His power always victorious.

The stories you will find here are not just stories of survival — they are stories of *Victorious Transformation...*

Stories of men and women who chose to rise up, take bold steps of faith, and move forward — even when fear was shouting loud and the way was unclear.

They trusted that the God who called them would be faithful to complete what He started. Indeed He was.

Maybe you are facing a battle right now. Maybe you are standing at a crossroads wondering if you have what it takes.

Let me speak this into your spirit: *You do — because God has called you!*

The dream He placed within you was not a mistake. The call on your life is irrevocable. The mountain before you is no match for the One who lives inside of you.

The Word of God says, *"For all the promises of God in Him are Yes, and in Him Amen, to the glory of God through us."* (2 Corinthians 1:20)

You are not forgotten. You are not disqualified. You are here on purpose, with a purpose, by Design — not by default.

So today, I declare over you: **You will rise. You will walk forward in boldness. You will step into the Victorious Transformation God has already authored for your life.** Every chain of fear is breaking even now. Every limiting label is falling off. Every God-breathed dream is being reignited.

This is your season to run. This is your time to shout. This is your moment to live fully awakened in victory!

Victory belongs to you — because victory belongs to Jesus.

Now step out, step forward, and step into the fullness of your *Victorious Transformation.*

BLESSINGS & LOVE,

Dr. Pamela Henkel

Real stories. Real battles. Real victories.

TABLE OF CONTENTS

Foreword by *Dr. Trunnis Goggins II* ....…….. pg 11

Stepping Into Your Victorious Transformation: The Pillars of
Christ-Centered Leadership *By Dr. Pamela Henkel* .... pg 15

Unbroken *by Sam Humphrey* .... pg 28

Altered Course: How COVID-19 Reshaped
My Life's Path *by Dr. Deidre Ann Calcoate* ....…........…… pg 49

If I can do this, so can you *by Ian Harvey* .... Pg 61

The Power of "Choice" *by Pele Hunkin* ....…........... pg 74

Portal of Possibility *by Dr. Amina Mohamed* ....….............. pg 86

Become Your Own Why *by Dr. Sheila Eggleston* ....…... pg 97

Reinventing The Best, You! *By Dr. Deborah Allen* ….…....…....... pg 113

Stepping Into Your Future Self *by Dr. Jodie Solberg* ….....……… pg 123

Beyond the Veil of Grief: Discovering Purpose through Loss
by Alanna Turtle ....…… pg 135

What Does the Next Best You Look Like?
by Dr. Donato Perricci ....…... pg 148

The First Step: Running into Infinite Possibility
By Dr. James Fomby ....…….. pg 158

A Different Kind of Voice *by Felicia Calcoate* ....…… pg 167

Rising Up From The Ashes Into Who I Was
Created To Be *by Megan Fortner* .... pg 174

From Brokenness to a Golden Repair *by Claudine Hicks* .... pg 184

The Power Of Faith *by Wilnord Louis Charles* .... pg 198

Embracing Joy in Your NEXT *by Nichol Perricci* .... pg 212

Beautifully Broken *by Bernice Johnson* .... pg 227

A Star Was Born: Embracing Self-Discovery
by Dalia Ganzel .... pg 238

Damaged Re-Branded *by Mildred Etherton* .... pg 252

Catapulted To Greatness (Unmerited Favour)
by Joyce Kamau .... pg 266

There Was Fear No More *by Carmen Cadena* .... pg 288

S.O. C.A.N. O.U. *by Sonya Howell Barrow* .... pg 304

Losing Me Finding I Am *by Denise Augustus* .... pg 314

Mirror Talk *by Karlita Green* .... pg 326

Final Thoughts *by Dr. Pamela Henkel* .... pg 336

FOREWORD
By Dr. Trunnis Goggins II

I n recent times, I experienced one of the most profound moments of my life: my son, Nick, enlisted in the United States Navy. As a father and a former service member, witnessing Nick follow in my footsteps filled me with immense pride and honor. Initially, Nick joined as a sailor, but he harbored a deep-seated ambition to become a Navy SEAL. For those unfamiliar, the SEALs represent the Navy's most elite unit and are among the most esteemed forces in the entire U.S. military. While Nick had already met the qualifications to serve in the Navy, aspiring to join such a distinguished group demanded more. The rigorous requirements necessitated that he push beyond his comfort zone, compelling him to evolve into his next best self.

When Dr. Pamela Henkel approached me to write this foreword, I was deeply honored. Participating in this anthology is a humbling experience, especially considering the esteemed individuals featured within these pages. These contributors have achieved excellence in their respective fields by daring to step outside their comfort zones, driven by an insatiable desire for growth. They recognized the existence of another level—a next best version of themselves—and were willing to work diligently and make sacrifices to attain it.

The narratives contained in this book are intended to inspire readers to embrace discomfort and take the necessary steps toward their true potential. This journey is not solely for personal fulfillment but also for the benefit of those who rely on us. The emergence of your next best self invariably serves as a beacon for others. Reflecting on this concept, I am reminded of my grandfather, Douglas Goggins Sr. In the mid-1930s, he was raising a family in Anniston, Alabama. Recognizing the possibility of a better life beyond his familiar surroundings, he ventured to Buffalo, New York—a city entirely unknown to him. Through divine guidance, relentless hard work, and a willingness to face the unfamiliar, he secured an improved future for his family, a legacy that has positively impacted his grandchildren and great-grandchildren.

The pursuit of becoming the next best version of oneself extends its benefits across generations. It serves as a source of inspiration to observers, including those who may not express their admiration openly. This transformative journey often entails significant sacrifices, as evidenced by the stories within this anthology. Some individuals have left behind friends and family, traversing the globe in their quest for self-betterment. Others have faced the heartbreak of loved ones turning away, unable to accept the evolving person they were becoming. Despite these challenges, these individuals remained steadfast, refusing to let anything or anyone impede their progress.

Reading the original edition of this book profoundly moved me. I felt a deep connection with the contributors, many of whom I have never met. Their experiences resonated with me, offering both benefits and blessings.

By choosing this book, you have acknowledged the potential for a better version of yourself. The authors within these pages offer guidance and inspiration to help you reach that pinnacle. Embrace their wisdom, and embark on your journey to becoming the next best you.

Trunnis Goggins, II PhD MBA
Author of
The 4Ps of You and
Visionary of the
Stories of…series
www.4ps-group.com

ABOUT AUTHOR

Dr. Trunnis Goggins II

Trunnis Goggins, II is a proud Navy veteran, educator, public speaker, visionary behind the "Stories of" book series, and host of The 4P's Podcast. Known for his message of Purpose, Plan, Passion, and Persistence, Trunnis draws from real-life experiences to inspire transformation in others. He currently resides in Asheville, North Carolina, where he enjoys life with his children and grandchildren and loving partner Dana. The 4P's of You reflects his commitment to helping people unlock their potential and live with clarity and conviction.

STEPPING INTO YOUR *VICTORIOUS TRANSFORMATION:*
THE PILLARS OF CHRIST-CENTERED LEADERSHIP
By Visionary Author - Dr. Pamela Henkel

I n a world that is shifting faster than ever, our understanding of leadership must be grounded more deeply than in strategy or skill. True leadership today is not about titles or achievements — it's about transformation. It's about becoming the person God has called you to be, so you can help others rise higher, too.

This chapter is not just about leadership; it's about the journey of *victorious transformation* — the kind that happens when we surrender fully to God's process and step out in faith.

Before we discuss the pillars of Christ-centered leadership — charisma, compassion, and ingenuity — let's first set our hearts on the transformation that lies ahead.

My Journey Toward Transformation

For over three decades, I have walked a path of serving others as a leader, mentor, philanthropist, and motivator of purpose. Yet the road was not always smooth. There were moments of uncertainty, moments of heartbreak, and seasons where moving forward felt impossible. Especially as a woman stepping into leadership, the obstacles were real.

But through it all, **God was faithful.** He placed mentors and leaders in my life — divine appointments who did not just offer advice, but invested their heart and wisdom in me.

They reminded me that leadership is not a ladder to climb — it is a mantle of service, and a life poured out for the glory of God.

It was through their example — and the relentless love of Jesus, the Lover of my soul — that I learned leadership is a transformative process. It is not merely reaching a goal, but becoming who God has destined you to be.

Today, I am honored to share the pillars that have shaped my journey. I pray they ignite your own victorious transformation, because **the same God who led me through every valley is leading you too.**

"For we are His workmanship, created in Christ Jesus for good works, which God prepared beforehand, that we should walk in them." — Ephesians 2:10

Step 1: Self-Reflection Through the Lens of Faith

The first step to transformation is honest, Spirit-led self-reflection.

Ask God to search your heart (Psalm 139:23-24). Invite Him to reveal not just your strengths but also the areas where He desires to bring growth.

This isn't a process of shame — it's a journey of hope. God corrects and directs because He sees the greatness He planted inside you.

"Examine yourselves, to see whether you are in the faith. Test yourselves." — 2 Corinthians 13:5

When you see your life through the lens of His truth, you can step forward in victory.

Ask God to reveal to you how He views you. You will be amazed!

Step 2: Establish Your Victory Goal

Don't settle for what seems *"possible."* Dream BIG with God.

Set an Ephesians 3:20, **Victory Goal** so bold that it demands you lean fully on His strength, not your own.

This is not about striving — it's about partnering with the Holy Spirit for a goal so great that only divine empowerment can bring it to pass.

What is God asking you to believe for? Where is He calling you to trust beyond what you can see?

"Now to Him who is able to do exceedingly abundantly above all that we ask or think, according to the power that works in us..." — Ephesians 3:20 (NKJV)

Your Victory Goal will stretch you, change you, and ultimately transform you into the leader God designed you to be.

The Three Pillars of Christ-Centered Leadership

1. Charisma: Holy Spirit-Led Influence

True charisma isn't about personality — it's about the anointing. It's the invisible pull of the Spirit at work through you, drawing people closer to Jesus, not just to you.

"Let your light so shine before men, that they may see your good works and glorify your Father in heaven." — Matthew 5:16

You are called to be a living testimony, radiating the hope, joy, and strength of Christ everywhere you go.

---

2. Compassion: Leading Through Love

Compassion is the heart of servant leadership. It is seeing people the way Jesus sees them — with eyes of mercy, patience, and hope.

"Finally, all of you, be like-minded, be sympathetic, love one another, be compassionate and humble." — 1 Peter 3:8

A compassionate leader reflects the Shepherd's heart. It's not about building your platform — it's about building people. Can I get an AMEN!

---

3. Ingenuity: Spirit-Inspired Creativity

Ingenuity is the divine creativity that turns obstacles into opportunities. When the world sees a dead end, Spirit-led ingenuity sees a door God is about to open.

"Call to Me, and I will answer you, and show you great and mighty things, which you do not know." — Jeremiah 33:3

As you lead, expect the Holy Spirit to give you fresh strategies, creative solutions, and bold new ideas.

Step 3: Seek Spirit-Led Mentorship

You were never meant to walk this path alone. God places mentors in our lives to accelerate our growth, correct our blind spots, and cheer us into our calling.

"Where there is no counsel, the people fall; but in the multitude of counselors there is safety." — Proverbs 11:14

Mentorship is a gift from God. Seek those who will point you to Jesus, not just to themselves. Be humble enough to learn, courageous enough to apply, and wise enough to pour into others in turn.

Step 4: Revisit and Evolve in Christ

Victory is not a one-time moment — it's a daily walk. Stay sensitive to the Spirit. Revisit your goals. Celebrate progress. Adjust when needed.

God is not asking for perfection — He's asking for persistence.

"Being confident of this very thing, that He who has begun a good work in you will complete it until the day of Jesus Christ." — Philippians 1:6

Stay in step with His rhythm. Transformation is a journey, and every step counts.

The Power of Gratitude in Your Transformation

Gratitude is a weapon of victory. It shifts your focus from obstacles to opportunities, from fear to faith.

"Give thanks in all circumstances; for this is God's will for you in Christ Jesus." — 1 Thessalonians 5:18

As you practice gratitude daily, your spirit strengthens, your vision clears, and you become ready to fully embrace your victorious transformation.

Your Victorious Challenge

Each day this week, set aside five minutes to journal three things you're grateful for —especially in the areas where you are trusting God for a breakthrough.

Watch how gratitude transforms your heart and enlarges your capacity for victory.

You are not here by accident. You are here on purpose, with a purpose, by Design — not by default.

The world needs your leadership, your voice, and your victorious story.

It's time to rise. It's time to walk in the fullness of your Victorious Transformation. Your Victorious Transformation begins now.

◉ Speak these out loud and let the Word of God strengthen your heart and renew your mind:

- **I am God's workmanship, created in Christ Jesus for good works.** (Ephesians 2:10)
- **I am empowered by the Holy Spirit to lead, love, and create with excellence.**
- **I am equipped for every good work God has prepared for me.** (2 Timothy 3:17)
- **I am not limited by my past; I am launched by God's promises.**
- **I have the mind of Christ and the heart of a servant.** (1 Corinthians 2:16)
- **I move forward by faith, not by fear.** (2 Corinthians 5:7)
- **I walk boldly into my victorious transformation because He who promised is faithful.** (Hebrews 10:23)
- **I am here on purpose, with a purpose, by design — not by default.**

- Victory is not just possible for me — it is already in motion.

Journal Reflection

1. What victory goal is God inviting me to believe for in this season?
   (Dream bigger. Write it down boldly.)

2. What obstacles have seemed too great — and how is God showing me that He is greater?
   (Shift your focus from the mountain to the Mountain Mover.)

3. What areas of my leadership and influence need to reflect more of Christ's charisma, compassion, or ingenuity?
   (Ask the Holy Spirit to highlight one pillar to strengthen this month.)

4. Who is someone I can ask to mentor me or walk alongside me in this next step of my victorious transformation?
   (Pray for divine connections.)

5. What am I grateful for today?
   (List at least three things every day this week. Speak them out loud.)

✿ Now Go out there and be the 🜂 and the 💡 everywhere you go.

Straighten Your Crown 👑

Dr Pamela

ABOUT VISIONARY

Dr. Pamela Henkel

Individuals seasoned with generous amounts of charisma, compassion, and undeniable essence possess the kind of ingenuity that shifts the world into its own greatness. The spirited professional, Dr. Pamela Henkel, is stewarding these traits in unyielding measure.

Dr. Pamela Henkel is an International Best-Selling Author, multifaceted compere, speaker, elite coach, CEO, and Founder of Purpose with Pamela and Pamela Henkel Ministries. Her multifaceted production and International radio conglomerate are fashioned to enthuse women, entrepreneurs, authors, and diverse professionals to take hold of their life's purpose. Dr. Pamela Henkel's mission is to add value to as many lives as possible. She reminds them they are here on purpose with a Purpose by Design, not by default. Partnering her passions with sincere regard for higher learning, community, and achievement, Dr. Pamela Henkel's career remains a reflection of creative grace, captivating the hearts and minds of many. She holds a doctorate in Philosophy, Christian Leadership, and Business and is on the Board of Regents for Cornerstone University.

Living life as one dedicated to the service of people, Dr. Henkel has maintained a nonpareil presence in the modern business world. As the creative founder of The Presigous Purpose Awards, The Pamela Show, and more, she extends her podcast, International radio, and social platforms to promote the voices of many globally. Her propensity for success in her field has led her to award-winning achievements, such as the nomination as one of the Top 50 Women of Business, an elite membership of the Power Voice, and personal mentorship from the world-renowned speaker and mentor Les Brown.

Dr. Henkel also received the Unsung Hero Award for helping people get the education they desire and deserve. Dr. Henkel's expertise has led to her positions as Elite Head Coach at the Million in You Academy and as an International

Speaker & Minister. She's also featured in the docudrama Think And Grow Rich Moms Rising, inspiring and empowering women to reach their full potential.

Dr. Pamela Henkel calls Minnesota home, where she enjoys spending time with her family and family pets. She cherishes the moments she gets to share with her loved ones. As well as always encouraging people to be the salt and the light everywhere they go.

Dr. Pamela Henkel. Leader. Energizer. Philanthropist.

Connect with Dr. Pamela

www.purposewithpamela.com

https://linktr.ee/Purposewithpamela

UNBROKEN

By Sam Humphrey

Life is unpredictable. One moment, you're standing in the spotlight, living the dream you fought for. The next, it's all stripped away, leaving you vulnerable, questioning if you'll even make it through.

For me, that moment came when I stood beside Hugh Jackman on the set of *The Greatest Showman*. A major Hollywood production, surrounded by some of the most talented people in the industry—it felt like everything I had worked for had led to this. But the truth? While I believed in God, I didn't *know* Him. My faith had taken a backseat to my career. I was consumed by success, stressed, and overwhelmed.

And then, everything changed.

Just months after standing in the Hollywood spotlight, I was lying in a hospital bed, hooked up to machines, my body failing me again. Crohn's disease had reared its ugly head, and while I didn't yet know the full extent of what lay ahead, I could *feel* the weight of something serious unfolding. The uncertainty was as crushing as the physical pain.

One moment, I was on top of the world. The next, I was fighting for my life.

But this isn't about staying on top or avoiding the lows — it's about *who you become* in between. It's about rising when you hit rock bottom, about how God is still there, even when you've drifted far. It's about the moments that redefine you.

So, let me ask you: **When everything is stripped away, what will your foundation be?**

Lying in that hospital bed, I found myself reflecting on the roller coaster my life had become. *The Greatest Showman* had shown me that no matter how many times life knocked me down, I could rise again. But now, reality hits harder than ever—life doesn't care about dreams or victories. It will test you in ways you never expected.

I'd fought my body and Crohn's disease before, but this time was different. The pain was unrelenting. The uncertainty, suffocating. It felt like being caught in a storm, helpless and powerless. I didn't know how I was going to make it through.

But one truth remained: when life hits, the only way forward is to keep moving. Take the punches. Get back up. Fight—not just in Hollywood, but in life. Resilience isn't about avoiding the struggle; it's about proving you're stronger than what's thrown your way.

Throughout my life, I've faced a choice: stay down or rise again. And each time, I've chosen to rise. But this time, it wasn't just about willpower. Lying there at my weakest, I was reminded of the faith that had carried me all along—the faith I had leaned on in the good times but nearly lost in the hardest moments. I had to trust it again. Even when I didn't feel it. Even when it seemed impossible.

That is when I realized—resilience isn't just about surviving the hits. It is about what you do after them. It is about leaning into a strength greater than your own, even when you feel distant or unworthy of it.

Looking back now, I see that the hospital bed wasn't the end of my story. It was the beginning of something bigger—a new fight, a new journey, a new chapter.

And that's what I want to share with you. Not just how I survived but how I got back up—step by step. How faith helped me move forward. And how it can help you, too.

FAITH IN THE FIRE: HOLDING ON WHEN EVERYTHING FALLS APART

I made it. I was in L.A., chasing my wildest dreams and

watching them come true. *The Greatest Showman* was a hit, and doors were opening all around me. For the first time, I felt unstoppable—like everything was finally falling into place.

Then, life threw me off course.

Isn't that just how it goes? We reach a high, only for something out of our control to remind us that we're not the ones writing the script.

It started with stomach cramps—sharp, relentless like my insides were being twisted and wrung out. Each wave of pain left me gasping, curled up, fists clenched, waiting for it to pass. But the relief never lasted. The nausea was relentless, and exhaustion swallowed me whole. I couldn't eat. I couldn't sleep. My body was failing, and I didn't even realize it.

At first, I tried to push through, hiding it from my sister and everyone else. I didn't want to be a burden. And honestly? I was terrified of hospitals. Needles were my biggest fear, and I would've done anything to avoid them.

I wish I could say I turned to God for strength, but the truth is, I didn't. Not because I didn't believe—just because I was too consumed by the battle in front of me. My world had narrowed to survival. One moment at a time. That was all I could manage.

Thankfully, my sister noticed. For three weeks, I told

myself it would pass, but it only got worse. Hiding it became impossible. She kept asking if I needed to go to the hospital, and though I resisted when the pain became unbearable— when I felt like I couldn't hold on any longer—I knew I had no choice.

Going to the hospital felt like surrender. But deep down, I knew the truth: If I didn't go, I wasn't going to make it.

Looking back now, I can see God's hand in it all—working through my sister, through my family, through every moment that kept me alive. At the time, it didn't feel like faith. It felt like survival. But maybe that's how He works—quietly, in the background, holding onto us even when we don't have the strength to reach for Him.

HOSPITAL STAY 1: THE DIAGNOSIS THAT CHANGED EVERYTHING

June 14 – July 8, 2018

The Diagnosis:

Walking into the hospital felt like stepping into another world— a sterile, disorienting maze of cold floors and white walls. The constant beeping of monitors was a reminder that life was fragile, each sound tethered to someone else's survival. The fluorescent lights were harsh, leaving no room for shadows, no space to hide. Time stretched endlessly as I waited for answers I wasn't ready to hear. The pain in my abdomen had become unbearable, and though we already knew I had Crohn's Disease, nothing could prepare me for the devastating news—a complete bowel obstruction. In that moment, the rest of my life faded into the background. There was only one thing to do: survive.

This hospital stay marked the beginning of a long battle that would stretch on for months, a war I'm still fighting today. My life became a revolving door of hospital stays, each one blending into the next.

The Fight:

The next three weeks were a blur of needles, NG tubes that made me gag, and a relentless regimen of IV fluids, TPN, and pain medications. The days felt like weeks, and the weeks felt like months. But what made it so excruciating wasn't just the physical toll. It was the uncertainty.

The doctors didn't just confirm my Crohn's Disease—they told me my condition was critical. Surgery was inevitable, and without it, I wouldn't survive. Those words felt like a punch to the gut.

Lying in that hospital bed, my body frail and my energy drained, I couldn't stop the flood of thoughts racing through my mind. Is this my life now? Am I destined to be trapped in this cycle of pain and hospitals? A part of me wanted to fight, but another part felt too exhausted to try.

Yet, even in the midst of the pain, exhaustion, and endless tests, I held on to something deeper. My faith in God, though not deeply personal at the time, became an anchor. It instilled a sense of peace and trust that this wasn't the end. I clung to the belief that there was a purpose in all of this, even if I couldn't see it yet.

There were also small moments of light—conversations with nurses who became companions and my sister, who was my rock through it all. She watched TV with me, cracked jokes to make me smile, and even slept in the hospital to remind me I wasn't alone in this fight. Those moments, though small, became lifelines.

The Road Ahead:

By the time I was discharged, I weighed just 58 pounds. My ribs and spine jutted out, my reflection a haunting reminder of what my body had endured.

But the battle was far from over—it was only just beginning. I wasn't done fighting.

Next came the surgery! But even then, I knew this fight was going to be an uphill battle—and I wasn't going to stop fighting.

That's when I met Dr. Beth Moore, a colorectal surgeon at Cedars-Sinai.

HOSPITAL STAY 2: THE SURGERY THAT CHANGED EVERYTHING

June 23rd – July 24th, 2018

The Decision That Changed Everything

The days after my discharge felt like a limbo—caught between home and the hospital. I still couldn't eat. The bowel obstruction hadn't resolved, and the only thing sustaining me was TPN—nutrition fed directly through my PICC line. It kept me alive but also tethered me to the place I thought I had escaped. I had left, but the hospital hadn't left me. What should have been a break felt more like a countdown—each day, a slow inhale, waiting for the inevitable exhale.

At my follow-up, the surgeons wanted to operate immediately. I can still hear their words: "It's a mess in there." Their urgency, though justified, felt cold—like I was just a case file, not a person. My sister and I felt it in our gut. Something wasn't right. We trusted that instinct, unaware that this single decision—seeking a second opinion—would change everything. Looking back now, I realize that decision didn't just change the course of my treatment—it quite literally saved my life.

That decision led me to Dr. Beth Moore, a colorectal surgeon at Cedars-Sinai—one of the most important encounters of my life. From the moment I met her, I felt something different. She wasn't just a doctor. She listened. She explained. She cared. There was no rush, no shortcuts—just careful, confident, unwavering attention to the details that could mean life or death.

Dr. Moore agreed to take on my case, carefully reviewing my condition and running a series of tests. She knew the risks of surgery were immense, so she focused on creating a strategy that would give me the best chance of survival. But then, one of the scans changed everything. The results were worse than expected. It was too dangerous for me to remain at home—if something went wrong, I could end up in emergency surgery with even fewer options. She admitted me back into the hospital.

The hospital had become a second home—one I never wanted but couldn't escape. The weeks leading up to surgery felt like a slow-moving countdown. I wanted it over with, but I also dreaded what came next. The contrast was staggering. Just months earlier, I had been standing beside Hugh Jackman on the set of *The Greatest Showman*, walking red carpets, attending premieres, and living my dream. Now, I was confined to a hospital bed, my world shrinking to sterile white walls and the quiet beeping of monitors.

But despite everything, Dr. Moore gave me something I hadn't felt in a long time—hope. She wasn't just trying to fix what was broken. She was thinking ahead, weighing every possibility. She developed a plan to manage the risks of the surgery I needed. My intestines were so inflamed that she recommended a temporary ileostomy to allow my body to heal before tackling the obstruction.

The Surgery and New Reality

September 6th. Surgery day. The last thing I remember: the mask, the sharp scent of antiseptic, the slow pull of anesthetic dragging me under.

When I woke up, everything had changed. A stoma. A colostomy bag. A foreign, overwhelming reality I hadn't prepared for. The physical recovery was brutal, but the mental toll was worse. I wasn't just trapped in a hospital. I was trapped in a body, a life that no longer felt like mine.

After a month in the hospital, I was discharged, but the struggle didn't end. The next six months were some of the hardest of my life. Adjusting to the bag, dealing with the stares, feeling like my life was on pause—it tested me in ways

I never imagined.

I wish I could say it got easier, but it didn't. Each day felt like a battle. I told myself this was temporary, but the weight of it felt permanent. My sister and I became amateur nurses, learning how to manage my TPN, flush my PICC line, and handle all the medical tasks that had become my new normal. At night, my colostomy bag was connected to a larger drainage bag so I wouldn't have to wake up to empty it. Even going to the bathroom felt like a pain—literally and figuratively.

My nurse, Norma, came weekly to change my PICC line dressing and monitor my labs. Despite our best efforts, I still developed a bacterial infection that led to sepsis—blood poisoning. I ended up back in the hospital to have the infected PICC line removed and replaced.

The Road to Recovery

Life doesn't always go the way we plan, but what's amazing is how much strength we find when we're forced to adjust. I wasn't the same person who walked into that hospital, but maybe that was the point. Maybe this was about rediscovering who I could become despite my circumstances.

Looking back now, I see it clearly: I wasn't alone in that hospital room. I wasn't alone in my darkest moments. God was there, holding me up, carrying me forward. And if He had me then—when I was at my lowest—why wouldn't He have me now?

HOSPITAL STAY 3: THE FINAL SURGERY

February 28 – March 18, 2019

The Waiting:

Through every moment of this journey, my family was my anchor. Their unwavering support kept me going when I thought I couldn't. Slowly, painfully, I began reclaiming my life. Though I was still healing, something in me refused to believe this was the end.

Co-hosting the New Zealand Attitude Awards in 2018 wasn't just a milestone—it was a test. A test of whether I was truly done. Despite everything, I wasn't. My sister held me up through the darkest times, and together, we pushed forward. I didn't have all the answers, but I knew my story wasn't over.

Yet, every day with the colostomy felt endless. The next surgery dangled ahead like a carrot on a stick—always close, never certain. The waiting wore me down. I remember messaging Dr. Moore:

"I can't hang in much longer unless surgery happens soon. In a few weeks, I'm giving up. No job, no money, haven't seen my friends in a year—I can't keep doing this. Please help me."

I longed for simple things—a sip of water, the freedom to leave the house without fear, to not feel like survival was my only purpose. Life had been reduced to counting every intake, every output, just trying to stay afloat.

I told myself everything always works out in the end. Maybe that was faith. Maybe it was just resignation. I wasn't questioning God, but I wasn't leaning on Him either. I believed in Him, but I wasn't seeking Him. My faith was more of an expectation—I figured I'd done enough to earn His favor that He'd just take care of the rest.

But today, I see it differently. Faith isn't just believing God exists. It's knowing Him, walking with Him, trusting Him beyond the assumption that things will simply "work out." Even when I wasn't seeking Him, He never left me.

The Surgery:

February 28, 2019 — I was wheeled into surgery for the second time in six months. The first had been about survival. This one was about reclaiming my life.

Being known worldwide as Tom Thumb from *The Greatest Showman* only amplified everything. My battle was no longer private. The media had caught on during my first surgery in September 2018, and suddenly, my fight was public.

"The Greatest Showman Star Sam Humphrey
Undergoing High-Risk Surgery."

The industry knew. The world was watching. But inside, I wasn't a headline. I was just a man facing the unknown — another surgery, another step into the abyss.

I trusted Dr. Moore, but the fear lingered. *Will I wake up? Will I have the strength to face what comes next?* As they wheeled me into the OR, unspoken thoughts crept in — *What if this is it? The last time I see my family, the last time I can tell them I love them.* I needed them to know.

Then the anesthesia took over.

The surgery was long. Complicated. When I woke, the bright lights and painkillers blurred everything — Dilaudid, Morphine, numbing the pain but not the awareness.

Then, I felt it. Or rather, I didn't.

The colostomy bag was gone.

In its place, a hole covered with gauze. A long incision ran down my abdomen, held together by 19 metal staples. Relief washed over me. I had made it through.

My sister was there. She had waited through every hour, refusing to leave. She was the first face I saw when I woke up.

The days blurred—nurses, doctors, machines. My body was weak, tethered to tubes. Every movement hurt. But I didn't care.

Because I was alive.

And I was determined.

The Road Back:

Even in those early days, my recovery surprised the doctors. My body healed faster than expected. But it wasn't just my body fighting—it was my spirit.

Still, doubt crept in. *What if this doesn't work? What if I never get back to who I was before?*

But maybe I wasn't supposed to go back.

When I finally left the hospital, I expected to feel nothing but relief. And I did, in part. The sterile walls, the fluorescent lights—none of it was my reality anymore. I was finally home.

But exhaustion settled in. Not just physical, but something deeper. For months, survival had been my only focus. Now, outside those walls, I was free—but I wasn't whole.

Crohn's wasn't over. It would always be there, lurking, waiting for its next move. But so would I.

I had made it this far. That had to mean something.

This battle had a purpose. I wasn't just rebuilding my career. I was rebuilding myself.

The world had tried to count me out. My own body had tried to count me out.

But God hadn't.

I am who I am today because of this journey because of Him.

And that's why I fight.

That's why I stand up for The Little Guy.

Because Jesus did.

And I always will.

YOU DECIDE

What does "The Next Best You" look like? It begins with one simple question.

Success isn't just the end goal but the journey—shaped by struggles, lessons, and growth.

We cling to the past, even when it hurts because the future feels unknown. But it is in those tough, unpredictable moments that we discover who we are.

For me, that moment came in a hospital bed, far from the dream of *The Greatest Showman*. From living the dream to fighting for my life.

If I can overcome that, so can you. Life tests us, but how we respond defines us. We all place faith in something. Where do you place yours?

For me, it's in God. If you're searching for answers, maybe it's time to ask: Could there be something greater than me?

So, what does "The Next Best You" look like? And how will you start today?

This is only a chapter in my story—one that is still being written. The full journey, from Hollywood to hospital beds and beyond, is one I look forward to sharing in my autobiography. But to truly understand where I am today, we have to rewind to where it all began—to the moment I entered this world already fighting.

Every battle, every setback, every moment of resilience has shaped me, leading me to where I stand today—and to a purpose far greater than I ever imagined.

If you're interested in learning more about my journey—what I've faced, overcome, and accomplished to make it to Hollywood, starring alongside Hugh Jackman in the Oscar-nominated and Golden Globe-winning The Greatest Showman—as well as my life after fame, my renewed faith, and everything in between, be sure to follow me on Instagram and my Instagram Channel.

Stay up to date on the release of my autobiography, upcoming speaking events, and the launch of my new company, The Little Guy Collective—coming soon!

ABOUT AUTHOR

Sam Humphrey

In a world where equitable representation is the main topic of conversation, in film/television, there are many individuals that seek to understand and speak on what diversity, inclusion, and disability empowerment representation means. Though very few can understand or match the authenticity, wisdom, and life experience on the same level as Sam Humphrey.

Sam's personal intention is to inspire people by demonstrating that no matter what your challenges or obstacles are in life, nothing is impossible. All you need is self-confidence, determination, a lot of hard work, and a single opportunity. Sam's hope is that he can empower you to achieve anything your heart or mind conceives. You can experience the most unforgettable moments and live life without regrets. Nothing can stop you.

Sam Humphrey is an Actor-Producer, RARE Advocate, and Motivational Speaker with his combined experience spanning more than ten years. Sam is famously known for playing the role of Tom Thumb in the feature film, The Greatest Showman. In 2020 he began working as a freelance development producer and now has a number of developed independent feature film/television projects in his portfolio. Since his breakout role in "The Greatest Showman," Sam has been frequently invited to speak about his accomplishments, time on-set, and advocacy work, focusing on mental health & disability awareness; while overcoming his own struggles and challenges to achieve success.

He began his career studying theatrical arts in high school, appearing in many on-stage productions (Midsummers Night's Dream as "Puck," Alice in the Wonderland as "Dormouse" and several others) and further studies at the "Australian College of Dramatic Arts." The Greatest Showman (Sam being a part of this film) won a Golden Globe for "Best Original Song" – THIS IS ME and was also Oscar-nominated for "Best-Picture" feature film. Sam has been mentioned in various media outlets, such as Vogue Magazine, Vanity Fair, and press interviews with major international news/media networks.

Currently based in Los Angeles, working as an actor producer, RARE Advocate, and public speaker, Sam enjoys keeping a healthy focus to artistically create a legacy that helps to change the world and leave it kinder, positive, safer, and full of love. "Failure isn't the end of the road; it's really the beginning."

Sam Humphrey ~ New Zealand & USA, Actor | Producer | Motivational Speaker | Author | Rare Advocate

Instagram: @thesamhumphrey | Facebook: Sam Humphrey

Instagram Channel: TheLittleGuyCollective

ALTERED COURSE
HOW *COVID-19* RESHAPED MY LIFE'S PATH
Dr. Deidre Calcoate

The COVID-19 pandemic, a global crisis that shook the world in unimaginable ways, reshaped my existence and set me on a truly remarkable journey. Within the chaos and uncertainty that engulfed our lives, I found myself at a crossroads. I made the audaciously bold decision to resign from my job and embark on the exhilarating path of entrepreneurship. Little did I know that this bold move would lead me toward unexpected success and personal fulfillment guided by the transformative power of the Divine. In this chapter, I will share with you how the pandemic, with its challenges and disruptions, has become a catalyst for profound personal growth and spiritual awakening. I will offer suggestions regarding how you can determine whether altering the course of your life is a viable option.

When news of the pandemic first emerged, I, like many others, never fathomed the profound impact it would have on every facet of my life. Our lives were upended, routines shattered, and fear permeated every aspect of one's existence. Fear and uncertainty lurked within every conversation as the future seemed shrouded in a dense fog. It was against this backdrop that I found myself at a crossroads, staring down the path of mediocrity or embracing the unknown. I turned to the wisdom of the Bible, prayers, meditation, brainspotting, and coaching - seeking solace and guidance in the face of adversity. I recognized the truth in Romans 12:2, which encourages us to "not be conformed to the pattern of this world but be transformed by the renewing of your mind."

The decision to leave a steady job that provided stability and comfort was not one I took lightly. However, as the pandemic raged on, my health declined, my motives were questioned, and it became apparent that the world was undergoing a massive transformation. I needed to get with the program. Clinging onto the past meant missing out on unexpected opportunities. It was time to take control of my destiny and forge a path that aligned with my passions and aspirations to support the healing of God's people. So, I continued my own healing at a much deeper level - healing past trauma and feelings of unworthiness. Embracing the vocation, the calling which was gifted to me at birth.

One of the biblical guidance's that resonated deeply with me during this time is found in Isaiah 41:10, which says, *"Fear not, for I am with you; be not dismayed, for I am your God; I will strengthen you, I will help you, I will uphold you with my righteous right hand."* This verse reminded me of the unwavering presence and faithfulness of Our Heavenly Father, even in the midst of tumultuous times. It inspired me to trust in His plan and to embrace the unknown with courage and conviction.

Thus, with fiery determination and a touch of trepidation, I bid farewell to my old life and embraced the exhilarating rollercoaster of entrepreneurship. In retrospect, leaving that position was the first step in sculpting a life that felt most authentic and invigorating.

Starting a business during a pandemic, some might argue, was irresponsible and maybe even seem irrational to others, an act of madness. The world is gripped by uncertainty, consumption patterns in flux, and the future remains shrouded in mystery. Yet, my body was in dis-ease amidst this chaos, and somewhere deep inside, I knew within the chaos resided a unique opportunity. The very cracks in the established order provided fertile ground for innovation and the birth of new ventures. It was precisely during times of upheaval that revolutionary ideas emerged, forever altering the trajectory of industries.

Starting anew during a pandemic may have seemed irrational to some, but I found solace in the promise of Romans 8:28, which assures us that *"in all things, God works for the good of those who love him, who have been called according to his purpose."* I knew that even in the face of adversity, God could bring about unexpected blessings and opportunities. With unwavering faith, I embarked on my journey, guided by

His grace and provision. Bolstered by a strong support system and a murky vision of my future, my pursuit of entrepreneurship began. I took leadership courses, learned to navigate social media, received an honorary doctorate, and worked with several life coaches.

The initial steps were fraught with challenges; ambiguity loomed at every corner, and doubts whispered in my ear with a persistent taunt. However, each obstacle became an opportunity for growth as I navigated unknown territory, eager to carve my niche. This mirrors the encouragement found in Joshua 1:9: *"Have I not commanded you? Be strong and courageous. Do not be afraid; do not be discouraged, for the LORD your God will be with you wherever you go."*

I designed a business model that utilized technology to meet the changing needs of a world affected by an ongoing crisis. Over time, my business began to gain momentum, attracting clients worldwide for my brainspotting and coaching services. My determination and adaptability started to yield positive results, pushing me onto an unexpected path of success.

As I upheld a commitment to excellence and a sincere desire to make a positive impact, I began to reap lucrative rewards. Each achievement boosted my confidence, and I recognized that the bold decision I made during the pandemic had catalyzed remarkable personal and professional growth.

VICTORIOUS TRANSFORMATION

My unwavering dedication to my newfound ambitions rekindled a passion and a sense of purpose that had remained dormant within me for far too long. The freedom and creative opportunities offered by my new venture breathed new life into my spirit, reigniting my zest for life, which had been dulled by the monotony of conformity and routine.

As I reflect on this life-altering chapter, I realize that the pandemic acted as a catalyst for transformation, pushing me outside my comfort zone and onto a path that resonated with my authentic self. It jolted me out of complacency, awakening a resilience and resourcefulness that had lain dormant within me. Through the fog of uncertainty, I discovered my true potential, and for that, I will forever be grateful for the trials and tribulations we endured during those unprecedented times.

In the end, the pandemic shattered my preconceived notions of success and stability, compelling me to forge a new path. By leaving my job and embracing entrepreneurship, I not only weathered the storm but also learned to dance in the rain. Rising from profound uncertainty, I emerged as a stronger, wiser, and more self-assured individual. With each step forward, I continued to build a life infused with passion, purpose, and prosperity, knowing that the challenges of the pandemic forever changed the trajectory of my existence.

In August 2023, I received an invitation to step into the role of Interim Executive Director at the Family Involvement Center (FIC), a family-run organization that had been integral in my growth as a young mother and wife. At FIC, I learned how to tell my story and how to use my lived experience to support others walking similar journeys.

For many years, I have maintained a close friendship with this organization. Having previously been employed by them and serving as an esteemed member of their board, my connection ran deep.

Initially, I had expected this to be a brief, three-month assignment. However, the Lord began to speak through others, sharing thoughts of a more permanent role for me. Despite my initial reservations, I recalled Isaiah 30:21, which reminds us that *"Whether you turn to the right or to the left, your ears will hear a voice behind you, saying, 'This is the way; walk in it."* Even though I was deeply committed to my current business venture, I could not ignore the divine calling.

With a sense of humility and obedience to the Lord's plan, I have accepted the permanent position of Executive Director as of this writing. This decision has been guided by faith and the belief that God's purpose often transcends our own visions and plans.

Whether you are contemplating a life change or a continuation of movement in the direction you are headed, I invite you to put God first as we are taught in Matthew 6:33: *"But seek first his kingdom and his righteousness, and all these things will be given to you as well."* Proverbs 3:6 encourages us to *"in all your ways submit to him, and he will make your paths straight."* By acknowledging God in all our endeavors and decisions, we allow His guidance to illuminate our path. Placing God first is not only a source of spiritual strength but also a compass for a fulfilling and purposeful life.

Other ideas you might want to consider:

1. Determine what you want to achieve in life.
2. Create a clear and inspiring vision for your future.
3. Set specific, measurable, attainable, relevant, and time-bound (SMART) goals.
4. Identify and challenge self-limiting beliefs.
5. Develop self-compassion and acceptance.
6. Cultivate confidence through small wins and positive self-talk.
8. Identify destructive habits that hold you back and create a plan to break those habits.
9. Surround yourself with positive and supportive people.
10. Embrace failure as an opportunity to learn and grow.
11. Take massive action.

As I journey towards becoming the next best version of myself, I am filled with anticipation to discover what the Lord has in store for me in this next chapter of my life. It brings to mind the lyrics of Tamala Mann's song, *"He Did it for Me,"* which beautifully proclaims, *"He did it for me, and He will do it for you."* I encourage you to take good care and always remember *Who* and *Whose* you are.

ACKNOWLEDGMENTS

I want to begin by expressing my gratitude to my Lord and Savior for the incredible work He is accomplishing through me. To my beloved family and friends, I hold you close in my heart, and I deeply cherish your unwavering support and encouragement. To all our readers, I extend my sincere thanks for joining us on this literary journey. It is my hope that you find not only joy but also enlightenment and a profound appreciation for the written word.

ABOUT AUTHOR

Dr. Deidre Ann Calcoate

This generation gesticulates a great need of benevolent leadership; those infused with empathic awareness, innovative resolve, and a compassion that supersedes the blaring chaos surrounding current culture. Fashioned with this exact ethic, is the enlivening professional, Dr. Deidre Calcoate.

Dr. Deidre is a Brainspotting practitioner, Transformational Life Coach, and the CEO and founder of Go Within Not Without, LLC; a multi-dimensional practice centered around reforming the intrinsic and emotional damages experienced by clients burdened by diverse traumas. Having experienced more than three successful decades of career experience in the public child welfare, juvenile justice, and developmental disabilities agencies, and more; Deidre is a reputable aid to all who undergo healing through her specialty.

Her mantra is simple: She is mandated to support the healing of others, so that they can thrive.

Owning an innate excellence backed by a profound mastery of self-actualization and overcoming personal life remonstrances, Deidre shares a deep regard for education, achievement, and communal involvement. She obtained a Bachelor's degree in Psychology from the prestigious Spelman College; as well as an Honorary Doctorate of Christian Leadership, from Cornerstone Christian University, in 2023. Having a natural propensity for sincere captaincy, Deidre has been widely recognized as a quintessential asset, in a myriad of humanitarian enthused vocations. Deidre was the first African American Bureau Chief, under the Department of Child Safety (DCS), in Arizona to oversee case management and permanency of children. She is also a Suicide Interventionist and has received elite training through several national organizations including The Annie E. Casey Foundation and The Casey Foundation, toward the effort.

Inspired by a passion to enkindle the masses into their intrinsic purpose, Deidre Calcoate has recently accepted the position of Executive Director of the Family Involvement Center. She has become a credible consultant to leaders in public child serving systems; a polarizing life propeller, orator, and a 4-time Bestselling Author and trainer, responsible for spearheading various program developments and encouraging peers to bequeath support amongst other parents involved in child welfare, juvenile justice, and developmental disabilities. Beholding an incredible aptness for altruism throughout society overall, Deidre has made it clear that she is mandated to bridge the gap between humanity and purpose; a trait she refuses to compromise.

When Deidre is not out making the world a better place, she is an asset to her local community and a loving member of her family and friendship circles.

Dr. Deidre Calcoate. Leader. Organizer. Philanthropist.

Connect with Dr. Deidre:
Www.gowithinnotwithout.com,
Facebook – Deidre.a.calcoate,
Instagram – dcalcoate2,
LinkedIn - https://www.linkedin.com/in/deidre-calcoate-gowithinnotwithout/

IF I CAN DO THIS, SO CAN YOU.

By Ian Harvey

Just imagine at the age of three you develop a health condition that will change your life forever.

At the age of three, I was diagnosed with acute psoriasis, a very visual autoimmune disease that was very difficult to understand as a child. During those early years, as psoriasis took hold, I missed a lot of school as the nurse called at our home to change the dressings daily. Psoriasis covered most of my body, and other children, in their innocence, were starting to make comments that were mentally difficult to deal with. Just imagine you go to shake someone's hand, and they quickly pull their hand back. It was very hard to come out of the dark corner and accept I will have this for life, and only I can decide to deal with the mental stress this caused.

I decided to take it head-on, and I refused to live in the shadows worrying about what people will think. In my mind, I got to a situation that was sink or swim.

Some 50 years later, I still have it, but I have programmed my mind to become unstoppable, focusing on what I do want rather than what I don't want.

Success is from within. Every single one of us can dream and live the life of our dreams, however, most of us tend to live within a paradigm of failure. The only person who can make you fail is yourself, but you must have the burning desire to be fired up from the inside.

Let me give you an example. I want you to imagine you walk through a garden in California, and it is a beautiful morning, the sun is shining, and you pick an orange off a tree. You bring the orange into the breakfast room and squeeze the orange, and out, comes apple juice. Do you really believe that you can do this? You pick your orange from a tree no one else has touched and receive apple juice from the squeezed orange. Do you really believe this can happen? You are probably saying you're crazy. Of course, this can't happen. However, if you were to squeeze yourself, what reaction would you get? Most people say, *"I am goal-orientated. I am focused-orientated. I am...I am...I am."* However, on the inside, the misery men are having their meeting in your mind. These are the people who give you doubts when you say, *"Hey, I'm going to do this,"* and then the little voice within says, *"No, you are not."*

These are the misery men (limiting beliefs)

They live inside of your head. They are there to disrupt you and your mind. They hold back so many people. They are like the quicksand crowd. Always doubting you and trying to put you off track. You must overcome these people.

The quicksand crowd is the people that say to you it can never happen, or it doesn't happen to people like you. These are the people who never achieve anything in their life and do their very best to make sure other people don't as well. They are also the people who waste your time and say get yourself a proper job. They say to go to a 9-to-5 job. Remember a job stands for just over broke.

The big question is how do you get rid of the misery meetings that go on within your mind? These meetings are what you need to counteract, stand up, and be counted against them. Most people just accept them and become part of the 95% of people who earn 5% of the wealth. The other 5% of the people earn 95% of their income. The question is why? The answer is quite simple. These 5% earn 95% of the money. They are the people that take the misery men on. They refuse to give in to them. They are the people that say I am going to get rid of these people from my mind. The question is, how do you take on these people? How do you get rid of the misery meetings that go on in your mind? You counteract. You read good books, set realistic goals, write them down, and have affirmations for breakfast. Every time the misery meeting says, *"Not a chance"* you say, *"Stop, stop,*

stop!" Speak it out loud, refused them and give them notice of eviction and say my mind is going to be full of positive affirmations. We're going to plant seeds of goodness. We are going to plant everything we can to uproot all of the weeds so that when we wake up in the morning, we feel fantastic. We do not have to battle the misery that lives in our minds.

At first, it will take some training. It's not one of those things where you wake up and say, *"Okay, today I'm getting rid of the misery men."* It takes time, and what you have to do is practice. Repetition. Repetition. Repetition. Keep on keeping on, and eventually, they will give in and will adhere to your eviction notice. Once your mind starts to get clear, you are going to smash goals like never before. If your burning desire is to be successful, then you need to make sure everything that goes in your mind is of value. Make sure no one is actually stealing anything from you including your time.

Official Notification

This is to advise everyone reading this… is giving formal notice of eviction to the misery men that live within our mind. We are no longer participating in the misery meetings, and your services are no longer welcome. Please leave our minds within the next 24 hours to avoid being hit by a massive wave of positive energy and belief in success.

Do you have what it takes?

I would like to take you back to when I was a child because that's when my burning desire for success began. Let me explain. I came from a family of six. My parents were hard-working; however, my father worked for the police force for the majority of his life. It was a time when it wasn't about money, it was about honour. So, although they loved us like any other parent would love their child, there was only just enough to go around. In the early years, I remember saying to my mother that I had a hole in my shoes and she said we'll put some cardboard into them.

We were not a wealthy family. Quite the opposite. I made the decision very early on that this was not going to be the lifestyle that I wanted for my future family. When I grew up, got married, and had children at a very young age, I decided I had to do something different. So, at the age of 12, I got my first job at a market store. I used to go to work before and after school. The guy who I worked for was a millionaire, and I shared with him my vision that when I grew up, I wanted a different lifestyle. I want to have plenty. I want to have everything in my life. He said, *"Well, it's quite easy. All you have to do is to set some goals."*

I had no idea what setting goals were all about, all I knew was that goals were something you kicked a football in. He said to me that you have to write down your goals, visualize what want, write it down, and that's the way you bring things into your life. So, I got a card, and I wrote down what I wanted from my life. Then, I waited, and I waited, and I waited. Really, nothing happened at all, and unfortunately, after a short period of illness, that guy died so I was still left in the wilderness thinking, how can I make a difference? How can I get a different lifestyle from what I was used to?

So, I continued to do some research to try and understand what this goal situation was all about. At the age of 16, I left school and I was told you know you're not going to make very much of yourself. *"What do you think you want to do?"* the Careers teacher said to me. *"What is it you think you can do because you really haven't been that attentive at school?"* So I said, *"Oh, it's quite simple. I am going to run my own business."* Then, the Careers teacher told me people like me don't run businesses, and that I would be best being a chef. Now, I can't even cook toast, so why would I ever become a chef? Now, don't get me wrong, there are some fantastic chefs out there, but that is not for me. I just decided not to take that option and instead start my own business.

I would get up at 5:00 AM, go to the wholesalers on a 50CC motorcycle, and buy watches to sell at the market. By the time I reached the age of 19, I was really in a great position because I had a booming business. The only thing I didn't have was any formal business acumen. I still didn't know how to run a successful business. I knew how to generate sales. I knew how to market products, but I didn't know how to run a business. As a result, I lost my business. I even went to live in sheltered accommodation. I went from top to bottom in a very short period. I remember lying on the cold floor with no furniture, having flashbacks of what the Careers teacher told me, *"People like you don't run businesses, become a chef,"* thinking, *No, No, No! This is not the lifestyle I want. I will get back up and do it again, again, and again until I make it work! Until I create the lifestyle that I want for my future family.* It's quite strange as Les Brown in his training sums up how I was feeling at that point in my life. He says, *"If you're falling in life, fall on your back because if you can look up, you can get up".*

I was actually there thinking, I know I have nothing in my life. I need to make a difference…I will make a difference…I am going to make a difference! I decided right then, and I remember the exact moment when I decided, it was time to get back up and stand proud. It was time to shake off the dust.

One of the first things that got me really confused was people telling me I had to think outside of the box. I searched forever to try and find this box. I could not find the box. I did not know what people were talking about. As I did more research into myself and my personal development, I realized the actual box does not exist. The box is just your mind that you are programming with things that can take you backward with negative thoughts of I can't do this or this is tough or thoughts people like me can't do things like this. Well, if you want the easy road you're probably correct, but what you have to remember is that 95% of the wealth goes to 5% of the people and 5% of the wealth goes to 95% of the people. Now, some people say it's 90/10 and that's fine, but the message here is 5% of people earn between 90 to 95% of all the wealth and the decision that you have to make for yourself is do you want to be part of the 5% that earn 90 to 95% of the wealth. If you do, the first thing you need to do is sort out this box in your head.

You need to actually understand it does not exist so you need to get hold of that box and throw it away, burn it, trash it, and just get rid of it. If someone says you need to think outside of the box, you should run a mile because you don't have a box. I always tell people who say to think outside of the box that I cannot because I don't have a box. There is no box. There are just limiting beliefs that you programmed into your mind. It's what makes the difference between success and failure. It's the thing that makes you put limiting beliefs and barriers in the way of your success. The reality is only you can put a limit on your success. You can have anything you want if you just want it badly enough. You know, when you are laying on a floor with no furniture, and you're looking up, you come to some fast conclusions.

I realized I needed to stay ahead of the game so I would invest quite heavily in training programs for myself. I also understood that to help as many people as I wanted to, I needed to invest in a mentor. I always remember one of the first programs that really touched my heart was from a guy named Zig Ziglar. He was a motivational coach, and he was absolutely phenomenal at getting across the message. The one thing he actually said was if you're going to be successful, you *have to pay the price,* and I knew what this meant. It meant I had to do the groundwork. I had to start setting goals. I had to start practicing affirmations. I just really had to raise my game so that I could help a broader spectrum of people. I had it in my heart that I needed to help a wide audience, and the only way I could do that was to invest in myself.

For me, it was quite easy. I was determined from that very day I had holes in my shoes and had to put cardboard in them. I made the decision then that when I grew up I was going to have a different lifestyle. I was going to give it my all to make sure that my future family would be taken care of as well as myself. I just wanted to give back. I wanted to go and find all the people that were in my situation that were thinking it doesn't have to be like this. I aggressively targeted people who were having a hard time. It's easy to find people who are having a good time and say would you like me to mentor you. For me, it was a case of let's go and find the people that really need mentoring. The people that really are trying to get up off their knees. I have built my whole career around helping people. I've never put anything before helping people because I've always known there's plenty to go around. But you have to go after it. You have to stand up and be counted. It has to be your time right now, and if you move all of your limiting beliefs and get rid of that box, then you can be as successful as you want. It really is up to you. I have helped hundreds of people transform their lives with my mentoring program, you could be next.

ABOUT THE AUTHOR
Ian Harvey

Ian Harvey's journey is one of resilience, vision, and transformation. Born into a bustling family of six children, Ian witnessed firsthand the sacrifices of his hardworking parents as they labored tirelessly to make ends meet. Their love was unwavering, but resources were scarce—instilling in Ian an early desire to create a different future for himself and the family he would one day lead.

At just three years old, Ian was diagnosed with acute psoriasis, a painful and highly visible autoimmune disease that marked much of his childhood. The physical and emotional toll of the condition was profound. Frequent absences from school and hurtful comments from peers made his early years especially challenging. Yet, even in the midst of adversity, Ian began to envision a better future.

With limited academic achievements and higher education out of reach, Ian turned to entrepreneurship. Armed with determination and a 50cc motorcycle, he launched his first business by the age of 18—rising at dawn to source products from wholesalers and selling them for profit. Within two years, his small venture had become a thriving business.

Realizing that success required more than hustle, Ian committed himself to personal growth. He sought mentorship and training, believing deeply in the power of self-investment. Under the guidance of his long-time mentor, Eric Vill, Ian quickly expanded his skillset and relaunched his business, reaching over £1 million in turnover within a year — and over $3 million within three. His efforts were recognized nationally when he was named *Runner-Up* in the prestigious **UK National Sales Awards**.

For over three decades, Ian has served as a trusted consultant and strategist to companies around the globe. His expertise spans:

- Product launch strategies
- Executive-level planning and leadership training

- Business turnaround consulting
- Personal development and performance coaching

His work has taken him to the USA, Japan, South Africa, and across Europe, helping both corporations and individuals unlock their potential.

Ian is also a recognized leader in the Direct Sales and MLM industry, known for motivating teams, increasing recruitment, and driving sales through proven programs and mentoring. He continues to mentor a growing network of entrepreneurs and professionals, sharing wisdom from his own hard-earned experiences.

Above all, Ian Harvey is a man on a mission—to equip others with the tools, mindset, and confidence to turn adversity into advantage and vision into reality.

Connect with Ian

FB: IanAHarvey

LinkedIn: ianAharvey

THE POWER OF "CHOICE"

By Fa'apepele Hunkin

The power of choice shapes destinies, carves identities, and defines who we are. I want to share the profound impact of the power of C.H.O.I.C.E. and explore its facets through Courage, Humble Heart, Obedience, I am Enough, Commitment, and Empowerment, the acronym I've used throughout my breathtaking journey. We make choices that affect our lives every day, knowingly or unknowingly. Everyone can choose whether small ones, like what to eat for dinner and what to wear to a retirement ceremony, or larger ones, like who to be your mentor and whether to leave a career to be your own boss. Every choice you make defines your experiences and contributes to where you are in life to be *your next best you*. It's an essential component of our self-development.

One of the benefits of having the ability to make powerful choices is that you can change your situation and your mind anytime if you don't like where you are in your life right now. Since you are in control, you can actively and purposefully pursue many possibilities for yourself. It's a consideration when deciding how to live a blessed and joyful life intentionally.

Make a brave choice intentionally that will make you proud. Making a choice entail leaving the known and entering the unknown. In life, it takes **COURAGE** to follow one path while giving up another. I have discovered how to embrace choice with courage as I develop, transform, and accept unexpected possibilities with God's blessings as I navigate the trials of life. Though it isn't always the easiest choice, the courageous choice frequently holds the key to releasing our true potential. Therefore, I chose to be better and not bitter about what life gave me when facing challenges.

After losing the Father of my children to a terrible accident in Ballad, Iraq, my Father to organ failure, my mom to a heart attack, and my brother to a brain tumor, I had to choose hope to have the courage to overcome life's obstacles. The loss of my loved ones was difficult for me to try to overcome. The brightness in my life seemed to have been supplanted by darkness, and I felt as though I had reached the limits of my faith. To get through the losses I endured, I needed to maintain that unwavering faith to make a powerful choice to stay strong for my children. I had to strongly believe in God and find the courage to do so because I have four lovely children to live for. I was inspired and motivated to continue by my steadfast faith in myself and God when I developed the courage to push through no matter what. One of my favorite quotes by John Maxwell states, *"Life is a matter of choices, and every choice you make makes you."* Therefore, I had to choose to be a strong mother and a warrior for my children to live a positive, blessed, and joyful life. I had to choose to be the better version of myself no matter what life was handing me. I did not allow what I was going through to define who I am. I love the better version of myself today!

I remarried ten years after the passing of my beloved Deanne Ignacio Tajalle, the Father of my children. Unfortunately, my marriage didn't last, and I experienced a divorce from my second husband that left me shattered. I didn't believe in divorce, so the only way I could hope to get through it was to keep fighting with everything I had to get back up. I hoped for a similar outcome in my marriage because my parents were together until they passed. I was so moved by the beautiful love my parents shared for one another. My favorite saying by my mentor Les Brown is, "When life knocks you down, make sure you land on your back because if you can look up, you can get up." I had to work hard to get back up and not let life's challenges keep me down. I understood it was OK not to be OK but not to stay shattered by life's challenges.

I am grateful for the pain I experienced in my journey, which gave me the courage to continue living. In addition, it blessed me with a **HUMBLE HEART**. A humble heart is the thread that connects our decisions in the magnificent fabric of life. Having a humble heart helps us remember how our actions affect us and the people around us. It encourages us to make choices with empathy and to take into account the requirements and viewpoints of others. We can better navigate the intricate web of life's options when we make humble decisions informed by an awareness of our limitations and a desire to learn from our mistakes. My grandmother and mother instilled in me that a humble heart will take me a long way, and I am grateful for their love.

I asked myself, *"What is your 'why'?"* Deep down in my heart and soul, I knew the solution. My main "*why*" are my children, my blessings, and my life. Even when I felt like giving up, my "*why*" was so powerful and motivating that it kept me going. As long as I have my kids, I can handle the hardships of life. My children and God's love, mercy, and grace kept me going when I wanted to quit so many times.

I never knew how strong I was until being strong for my children and myself was the only choice. I encourage you to fight back, don't quit, and don't give in when your "*why*" is more powerful than that punch. Remember that giving up is not an option!

I learned **OBEDIENCE** to God's calling throughout my breathtaking journey and my best choice. To obey God, first, I had to be receptive to hearing His voice and pursuing His will for my life. That entails bringing Him into every arrangement, scheme, and dream I have. I continuously seek God first and do not hesitate to invite Christ into my life for Him to transform me completely. It is sometimes unsettling because I worry, *"Well, what if He doesn't agree with what I do?"*

I've concluded throughout my breathtaking journey that whatever God has in store for me is superior to anything I could have imagined. Being obedient to His calling in my life has been my best choice.

Whatever your circumstance, simply requesting God's guidance and praying for His will in your life will clarify things considerably. If you're praying about something, it's probably from God, and the scenario gives you long-lasting serenity. Conversely, if something is causing you anxiety or strife rather than calm, perhaps it's time to let go, even if your heart tells you otherwise. Learn to let go and let God because He has an excellent plan for your life. I've concluded that, just like you.

However, do not be deceived; obedience to God takes time, even when your emotions and heart tell you otherwise. The more we seek after Christ via prayer and the Sacraments, the more graces we get that give us the strength to let go. Realizing Christ is in control, we grow to give up our feelings and desires in favor of Him. I encourage you never to let anyone change your heart from God's calling. The most empowering moment in your life is when you take control of it. You make positive decisions based on what you want and need, not what others want and need.

It took my divorce to FLY-First Love Yourself and accept that **I AM ENOUGH**. As I looked over my life, I realized that although I have made progress, I have yet to do it as quickly as I wanted to make progress. But it still counts! For the first time, I believed that I was enough. It's one thing to say, *'I applaud all my little accomplishments.'* It's an entirely different thing for me to believe I deserve all of God's blessings over my life. And for the first time, making the powerful choice to take charge of my life and own my story was enough. It's a beautiful feeling and the best choice I have made. I am grateful to God for His precious love, mercy, and grace that carried me this far. His grace is sufficient for me.

I made many mistakes, and I never stopped trying to better myself. I have learned to embrace all of my imperfections that molded me into the imperfect me for me. Acceptance in life doesn't mean you should stop trying to improve yourself. There is a refined but significant difference. You will never have enough, no matter how much you get, and you will always feel *"less than"* since your value will depend on whether you achieve what you believe you lack. If you strive for more without accepting yourself without what you think you lack. By taking yourself as you are right now, you can and will continue to work toward growth, but it will come from a place of wholeness rather than insufficiency. You will undoubtedly be drawn toward growth and expansion once you can genuinely accept the idea that *"I am enough"* since that is what human nature is. But you'll go from there. I encourage you to believe in yourself because I believe in you and know you are enough, and I AM ENOUGH. We are enough!

Through my journey, **COMMITMENT** is the foundation of a powerful choice. Committing myself to God's calling in my life was life-changing. The more I showed up for myself and put in the work, the greater my sense of success. However, there were times when things got tough, and it was all too easy to fall out of that commitment. I sometimes realized that I was not truly committing to my life when I only did what I said I would do when things were easy.

It is the unwavering commitment to following our chosen paths despite challenges. Challenges are a part of any choice we make in life, and dedication gives you the resiliency to face them head-on. When we commit to a course of action, we provide meaning and purpose, assuring it will eventually bring fruit. It took a lot of commitment to my commitment to get to where I am today.

The ability to do what was right to be my next best you were the key to **EMPOWERMENT**. I chose to be the change I wanted to see and not what others wanted to see under pressure because I dared to persevere and be great. I consciously decided to achieve greater heights God has in store for me. I was empowered to tell my story and share God's glory with my HEART OF A WARRIOR-The Humble Journey of a Samoan Warrior best-selling book. I must admit that I will never doubt what God has created in me and born out of me because He is my life's sole author and finisher.

Our journey will always have obstacles, and life is full of trials. The most empowering paths to success come through failed experiences. Take what you can from the experience, get back up, and move on.

I permitted myself to step into my greatness and confidently stepped into it with faith, joy, and lots of love. I had to trust the process and believe everything would work according to God's timing. I want you to believe that choosing to better yourself is worthwhile.

Realizing that we are the ones who compose our own life's story is crucial. Every choice, no matter how small or significant, affects the course of our story. By accepting this empowerment, we can transform from mere observers to active designers of our fates. By making choices, we may overcome constraints, realize our full potential, and design a life that resonates with authenticity and meaning. Authenticity is everything in my breathtaking journey, and I am free to be the beautiful, authentically me God created me to be.

I am here to empower you to use your inner strength, love, faith, and commitment to improve yourself. Live a life of delight that I call the *"unspeakable joy of the Lord."* As a single parent, I am a source of physical and emotional support for my children. I had to empower myself after my loved ones passed away to provide a stable atmosphere for my children. The value of having a family in life can't be overstated because life is what you make of it. Be empowered and keep giving the world strength by being your unique self.

The painful experiences of losing a spouse, especially my parents, and then a divorce were substantial life lessons, and I am grateful for them all. I gave myself the most incredible gift—to love the person God created me to be, *"the beautiful authentic me."* I loved myself enough to change for me and be what I wanted in this life, not what others wanted to see. The bold and unique person in the mirror, which is me, inspired me! The one constant thing was my desire to rise and exceed my expectations for my blessed life. I tend to fall when times are rough, but I always choose to get up. I learn, grow, and rise to greater heights because my God is bigger than my problems.

It has been a truly amazing experience to learn to accept and love myself. I became aware that when I took control of my life, I started to appreciate my new self and expand my self-worth. I finally understood that my superpower and strength came from within my heart. I am grateful for the tremendous spiritual and emotional journey I have been on because of my personal development and the power of choice to be the author of my life. I permitted God to serve as my foundation, as He is the sole cornerstone of me and my children's lives. Despite my losses, setbacks, and divorce, I had to look for the silver lining to move forward and handle the situations I've experienced with grace and so much love. With a grateful heart, I have grown gracefully through grief and life's challenges.

I inspire you to learn the importance of being conscious of your choices to succeed and be *your next best you*. Also, remember to use your power of choice effectively. As we navigate life's complex web of options, remember the acronym CHOICE: courage, humble heart, obedience, I am enough, commitment, and empowerment. Knowing who you are and what values you uphold gives you a solid foundation on which to base your decisions on approaching obstacles in life. The choices you make are more prosperous, deeper, and more satisfying. Believe that you are acting in the highest regard. This is the beauty and power of having a choice to be *your next best you*.

ABOUT AUTHOR

Fa'apepele Hunkin

Fa'apepele Hunkin is from the beautiful island of Samoa and is affectionately known as "Pele," which means "Sweetheart" in her native Samoan language. She owes her faith, life, and breathtaking journey to her ancestors, who made the ultimate sacrifice and paved the way for her and her twelve siblings. Pele is a devoted mother of five loving children: she birthed Nicole, Dean Jr., and Victoria. God blessed her with two more by heart and love, Dominique and Isabella, granddaughters Milan and Nalani, and fur baby Deabo. She is a retired United States Army Combat Veteran, a single parent, a widow who remarried, and now a divorcee.

Today, Pele is a survivor of many losses, a dynamic speaker, an international and best-selling author of her book HEART OF A WARRIOR, The Humble Journey of a Samoan Warrior, co-author of eleven anthologies, and founder of Pele Inspire-Embracing Authentic Love. She is also a National Campaign Team Member and Alumni of the Wounded Warrior Project and has been included in STRATHMORE'S WHO'S WHO WORLDWIDE 2022 EDITION.

Pele is a certified Power Voice global speaker, having been trained to speak by the world-renowned Global motivational speaker Dr. Les Brown. Pele's apparent oratorical skills were showcased during the Les Brown Power Voice Summit, where she was a featured speaker. Pele's ability to candidly share her inspirational story with others through her books and speeches has truly blessed her with inspiring, empowering, and impacting of those she encounters. She challenges others to say and do everything with love and from their loving hearts. The two words she lives by daily are LIVE and LOVE.

Connect with Pele

Website: www.peleinspire.com
Email: pelehunkin03@gmail.com
FB: www.facebook.com/peleinspire FB:
www.facebook.com/pelehunkin04
IG: www.instagram.com/peleinspire

PORTAL OF POSSIBILITY

By Dr. Amina Mohamed

The lips of wisdom are sealed except to the ears of understanding - The Kybalion

It all starts with a thought that changes your life; you might hear it as a whisper or see it as a sign. But you have known for a long time that there was a yearning in your heart for more. Some call it desire; others say it is your soul-seeking expression. Only you know what it means to become the next best you.

You have to be willing to say yes, regardless of the fear inside you. I might not know you, but here's what I know about you already. I know that life hasn't always been fair; you may have failed and fallen down many times. You are probably starting to think that things don't work out for someone like you. But I am here to remind you that the impossible is just an opinion, and it certainly doesn't have to be yours.

When you make a decision, it is the triggering mechanism that starts to grow inside you. You realize that you were only stagnant because you haven't been clear. You see, your real life is the one you keep imagining. It is the life that you weren't given, but it is the one you deserve. There are many successful people in the world, or what may be defined as success, that all started where you are today. A fleeting moment where an idea, thought, or vision for a greater life begins to spark.

As you read this chapter, remember that this is your moment to allow your heart to find healing, purpose, and, most importantly, activation. When I speak of the heart, it is not the one that fiercely pumps blood through your body to keep you breathing but the subconscious mind, which is the doorway to prosperity. You may have already found your purpose, or you might be in the process of discovery, but I want you to follow me on this journey as we enter into the heart portal of possibility, where you will discover how and what it means to truly find your next best you. Your Higher Self has been awaiting this moment, and now is the season for your ascension.

This portal is not like anywhere you may have been before. It is the direct realm that connects you to the Divine. It is the communication centre of the Infinite Power that has always been within you. As you continue on this chapter, stay open to receive the direct downloads and inspiration you need to reach your next best you. This portal is a place within you that has been given to you by a Higher Power. It is the roadmap that will guide you to what you really, really want in life if only you *feel* it.

Just as Abdullah taught Neville Goddard, *feeling is the secret*. You have to begin to think feelingly about your future so that you can manifest it into reality. You see, the Universe has many laws, and whether you know the laws or not, you will be held accountable. It's like when your mum asks you to do something, and you forget to do it until she comes through the door. You know she will be upset even if you do it at that moment because the timing is everything. Every action has a consequent effect on your internal and external world. This means that the law always applies and that the absence of knowledge is not a defence. The law of all laws is the law of cause and effect. It is the very planes of living that mould the world that will shift you into your dream life and that will open the abundant flow of life towards you.

This law states that every action will produce a reaction. For example, if you open your window on a hot summer's day, the cool breeze will flow in and allow the air to circulate. Your action of opening the window *caused a like effect* in your desire to cool down your body temperature. This is the same with your thoughts; when you decide the image of what your next best will be, it will cause a similar effect to what you feelingly think of in your mind. The clearer the image, the better your results in achieving your desire.

The magnitude of your life is so important that the Divine has placed you here at this time. There is no such thing as chance, luck, or coincidence. You were chosen, and in turn, you also chose. Now, in order to apply these principles, you will need to use the DAC Cycle from #1 Amazon Best Seller,

The Confidence Catapult - How to ask for what you want and get it. This revolutionary new thought strategy will help you take a quantum leap from who you are now to who you have always wished to become.

Step 1 - Define

The first step is to define. This means you clearly define what it truly looks like to become the next best you. As Solomon said, *"Where there is no vision, the people perish."* I want you to go to that place in your heart where you have locked your dreams. Open the door, and allow what you really really want to flow through you. It has to be a goal that will take you somewhere inside yourself you haven't been before. You have to truly want it and want it badly. Most people move from two places in their lives, inspiration and desperation.

Today, I want you to move from inspiration so that you can begin to create the life you desire. Your wonderful, magnificent mind thinks in pictures, so what is the image you are holding on the screen of your mind for the next best you? Does it look like a new lover? Does it mean starting a business? Does it mean investing in your health? I want you to pause and reflect on this next question - *if you knew you were being supported, what action steps would you take?*

Breathe in, breathe out, and listen for the answers.

Write it down and move in inspired action.

Step 2 - Align

The second step is to align. Now that we have defined who we want to become through purposeful intentions, we can align with that version of ourselves. When you look at the definition of alignment, it means the proper position or state of agreement. When we align to our new way of being, what we are really doing is aligning our inner truth. This is about remembering the uniqueness of who you are. You are not here to compete with anyone, but you are here to create. When you shift your perspective to this creative state, you embody an energy that supersedes. With God, you co-create the life you truly dream of. You don't have to wait for heaven or be completely sinless to earn your dream. You must simply align with the inner voice of the person you wish to become. What conversations would they have? How do they show up every day? What habits do they have? A shark in a fish tank can grow eight inches, but the same shark in the ocean can grow to six feet. This is your time to reach your full potential and remove the mental bondage that was holding you hostage.

Repeat this mantra with me: "Lack is an illusion, lack is an illusion, lack is an illusion."

Step 3 - Create

The third step is to create. You cannot have any change in your life until you embrace the change you seek to experience. Life always speaks to us, and the lesson is repeated until we learn it. Now that you have your clear desire of who you want to become and have aligned your inner speech to become that person, you will need to move into action and create. There are only two ways to create. This is with your words and your actions. Sometimes, this action will come to you in a spark of inspiration; you will find that you are doing something, and suddenly, a moment of genius overcomes you. Listen to that voice, and write down what it says. Other times, you have a clear roadmap of what you know you need to do. Despite how you have been conditioned by your past experiences, it is time to wipe the slate clean for your next best you to enter. Instead of the self-loathing cycles of procrastination, anxiety, and fear, I want you to free yourself and use that wonderful imagination. You have already been using it against you when you have imagined the worst, but it is now time to use it for you and start believing in your portal of possibility. Remember, you are not the observer of your reality but the co-creator, and with God, Divine, Source, all things are possible to those who believe. My favourite book says, *"It is the believers who will be successful."*

Pause, take a deep breath again, and start thinking about that desire you have within you. When you have the feeling of joy flowing through your body, and you feel your energy shifting, then ask, *"Higher Self, what is the next step for me in this moment?"*

Listen, write it down, and move into immediate action.

When I was sitting on my best friend's bedside in a cold hospital room, the faces of despair were all staring back at me.

I could feel the helplessness in the room that echoed so loudly. In a faint voice, she whispered, *"Amina."*

As the words filled the room, I felt the speed in my body rush to her help before my mind could think. There wasn't much I could do now, but I felt in my heart that I was being called.

"Amina," she said again. I stared back into her frail stature and smiled. She pulled me in closer and said, *"Pinky Promise."*

My immediate thought was that this was not the time or place for childish games. But there was a seriousness in her tone, so I entertained this idea. She raised her pinky finger, and I interlocked it with mine. Then she whispered, *"Pinky Promise, no regrets."*

As my eyes started to flood with tears, I felt the sharp pain that was really pressing on her mind as she transitioned. I smiled and said, *"I Pinky Promise, no regrets"*.

It was at this moment that I remembered the words of my mentor, Mr. Les Brown, *"Live full so you can die empty."*

It was evident in this moment that although she had come to the end of her life on earth, she felt she hadn't lived her life. It was the *"what if?"* questions that were the loudest. The pain of regret is the curse of a half-lived life. What if you never discovered that next best you? What imprint would you be denying the world? What impact would be starved from our existence? What idea would you imprison within you if tomorrow never came?

I want to leave you with this: You are more powerful than you know, and they fear the day you find out. Your next best you is waiting to be birthed through; don't deny the world of your magnificence because you were too afraid, too doubtful, or too alone. It is time to truly live full so you can die empty. You are an open channel for the divinity within you that is calling to be seen, heard, and experienced. You are not reading this book by accident but with purpose and intention. The world is seeking your contribution; what will you bring forward, my love?

Your Sister in Prosperity & Possibility

Amina Inspires

ABOUT AUTHOR

Dr. Amina Mohamed

Dr. Amina Mohamed is a highly acclaimed Success Coach, TEDx Speaker, and Publisher, renowned for her extraordinary ability to empower individuals to unleash their full potential and activate their greatness DNA. With a passion for helping both entrepreneurs and students, Amina has dedicated her life to enhancing self-confidence, eliminating mental blocks, and optimizing performance in order to facilitate transformative personal and professional growth.

VICTORIOUS TRANSFORMATION

Amina's journey to success has been nothing short of remarkable. Her inspiring work has not only earned her recognition within her field but also numerous prestigious accolades. She was honored with a nomination for Influencer of the Year by the esteemed Black Muslim Awards, a testament to her impact in the global community.

As a Global Peace Ambassador affiliated with the United Peace Federation, Amina is on a profound mission to liberate individuals from mental and emotional bondage. She envisions a world where true freedom reigns, and she actively collaborates with the Commonwealth Entrepreneurs Club to foster greater cooperation in competitive spaces.

Amina's commitment to her mission extends far and wide. She was also the featured guest speaker at the Om & Bass WellBeing Festival with over 3,000 people. Amina was able to set the stage for a harmonious and transformative experience for all attendees in the co-collaborative effort for spiritual spaces.

Furthermore, Amina has been a featured guest on local newspapers including a feature guest speaker at the Houses of Parliament. Her reach and influence extend beyond the digital world, allowing her to connect with and inspire individuals in her community and beyond.

As an accomplished author, Amina's book, "The Confidence Catapult - How to ask for what you want and get it," reached the pinnacle of success as a #1 International Best Seller. Her literary accomplishments have expanded into coaching, where she now guides aspiring authors and entrepreneurs on their journey to becoming Amazon best sellers through her coaching and publishing company.

Recently, Amina's contributions to world peace were recognized with the prestigious award of an honorary doctorate, a testament to her dedication and unwavering commitment to making a positive impact on the global stage.

In essence, Dr. Amina Mohamed is a beacon of hope and inspiration, dedicated to helping individuals discover their innate gifts and harness the power of their subconscious minds to create the lives they truly desire. Her vision is simple yet profound: to bring out the best in everyone and to make dreams come true. With Dr. Amina as their guide, individuals around the world are empowered to reach new heights of personal and professional success.

Connect with Dr. Amina

www.aminamohamed.co.uk

BECOME YOUR OWN WHY

By Dr. Shelia Eggleston

om, I have a question for you? Whatever we needed, whatever we asked for, or whatever you wanted us to have, you never let anything or anyone get in the way, you were like Super Mom and we were your *"why"* that gave you superpowers to make it happen. You made it happen, Austin and I have graduated from college, started our careers and moving out of town. We are who we are because of the Mom you were, and oh Dad too (*smile*). But more importantly, what happened Mom? Where's the person you were? *Why are you not to yourself, what you were for us?*

I intentionally would not give Chelsey an answer, it was too painful. I had just lost my mom who was my best friend and my cheerleader, to cancer the year before and now my children (my world) were leaving me. While I was the most proud Mom that you could have ever met, I was the saddest as well. For years, my life revolved around my children, Chelsey and Austin. From the moment they were born, they became my *"why"*—the reason I woke up every morning, the reason I sacrificed, the reason I pushed through exhaustion, and the reason I found joy in the smallest of victories. They were literally my miracle babies, but that's for another story. Their needs, their dreams, and their futures, *literally gave me life*, I was living life through them.

A few weeks later, I was attending an online seminar and the guest speaker said *"maybe it's time to change your why"*. I felt like the speaker was speaking directly to me, the only thing he didn't do was call me out by my personal name. It hit me like a ton of bricks, it was a wakeup call, all at the same time. My *"why(s)"* Chelsey and Austin no longer needed me to be That Mom, but I needed me, I needed me to **become my own why.**

For so long, my identity was wrapped in being Chelsey and Austin's mom. It was the most fulfilling role I had ever known, but I had never prepared myself for the day I would need to change my why(s) and **become my own why**. I had poured all of myself into raising them, loving them, and guiding them—so much so that I hadn't considered what would happen when they no longer needed me in the same way. The emptiness I felt wasn't just about their absence; it was about the loss of purpose, I hadn't realized was so deeply tethered to them.

At first, I filled the silence with busyness. I dove into projects, even created projects that didn't need to be created, reconnected with friends, found retail therapy, and new ways to stay occupied. But make no mistake, distraction is not purpose. And in the quiet moments, I still felt the ache of a question unanswered, What now?

Becoming my own why was not an overnight revelation. It was a journey — one that required me to sit by myself, with myself, to embrace the discomfort of self-exploration, and to recognize that I was more than the role I had played for so many years. It meant discovering who I was outside of being a mother. It meant acknowledging my own dreams, passions, and desires that, truth be told, I allowed others and myself to place them on the back burner.

I remember a time when my daughter needed encouragement to apply for a study abroad program in college for part of a semester in Paris. I told her to believe in herself, that she was strong, capable, and worthy of success and remember life and death is in the power of our tongues and we choose to speak life, we declare and decree you will be accepted. The words and my belief came so easily when I spoke them to my daughter, in fact she was accepted into the program and had an amazing experience studying abroad in Paris.

But as I stood at the crossroads of my own transformation, I realized I needed to speak and believe those very same words for myself. I began to reflect on what had always brought me joy. What made me feel alive before my world was centered around my children? What did I once dream of that I had put aside, put on the back burner? Slowly, I started leaning into those questions. I allowed myself to dream—not for my children, not for my husband, but for myself. I had to tell and convince myself, *"Shelia, this is not selfish, it is necessary."*

A Transition into Possibility

The journey to **becoming my own why** meant I had to intentionally and unapologetically choose me first! This was a challenge which became my life journey.

Becoming my own why required me to pursue my own personal motivations, passions, and goals in life, take ownership of being my own driving force and understanding what truly inspires and motivates me and be accountable to myself to take actions that align.

Becoming your own why, meant turning inward and asking, "What ignites my soul?" It's about recognizing that even after fulfilling the needs of others, you remain a wellspring of dreams, passions, and untapped potential. I allowed myself to dream—not for my children, but for myself.

Embracing the Gift of Reinvention

I realized that for years, I had taught my children to chase their passions and dreams, to believe in themselves, to find purpose in their own paths. Now, it was my turn to take my own advice. If I wanted to live a life that was full and meaningful, I had to step into a new identity—one where I was not just a mother, but a woman with her own passion, dreams, and purpose.

The empty nest is far more than an ending—it's a metamorphosis. With more time on your hands, you have the unique opportunity to explore parts of yourself that may have been overlooked or sidelined. Whether it's reconnecting with a long-forgotten hobby, pursuing a new career interest, or simply finding joy in the little moments of every day, this period is your blank canvas.

Imagine this…every quiet morning with a cup of coffee, every leisurely walk in nature, is a chance to rediscover what makes you uniquely you. The discipline, love, and resilience that once nurtured your children are now the very tools that can help you shape the **Next Best You**.

Commitment to myself

Self-reflection: Imperfect says I'm perfect. It's time to embrace everything you are—and everything you aren't. This involves heart-searching to understand what truly matters to you, what brings you joy, and what kind of impact you want to make in your world. Knowing who you are and embracing it in all aspects of your life grounds you and helps you to build a strong foundation. We can't expect to change ourselves if we don't know where we are in life and where we are starting from, in the first place.

To make a lasting change, the process starts when you recognize who you are and make a decision to love that person and choose to pursue something more deserving for yourself. This phase is a huge step. It's now your chance to come to terms with the person you are and realize that you have the power to choose who you are going to become.

When we align our actions with our principles, our confidence boldly steps forward. This confidence will elevate your decision to take action and become our own why.

Authenticity: You were bold enough to take the first step; the second step takes courage—courage to be authentically you. Who are you really? To **become your own why**, you must live a life that aligns with your true values and beliefs, not societal expectations.

Live your life with passion. Knowing your "*why*" puts you in touch with your passion. You will live your authentic life and do what you love. All of your goals will be infused with this same energy to produce amazing results.

You are inspired enough to tell yourself that no matter what has happened before this point, you are ready to be uniquely and authentically you.

Taking action: Now that you have identified, you are your *"why"*, you must actively make choices and take steps to live in accordance with your new *"why."* Your *"Why"* is yours and yours alone. Without a *"why"*, you end up living your life for others.

Without your own map, you will find yourself lost and other people will drag you along on their journey. You may find yourself on this journey trying to please others or living out a life script you've been handed.

When you **become your own why** you own what you are doing. You do it all for yourself. Make the commitment to yourself, now is the time to show up for you and follow through for you. The chance to transform and elevate your life starts with a single commitment.

Get to know your "why" (yourself) better. Ask yourself... *"What am I passionate about?", "What makes me happy and feel fulfilled?", "What positive change do I want to see in my world?"*

Your "Why" Motivates You. Your *"why"* is the driving force that keeps you going and helps you stay motivated when things get tough.

Your "Why" Keeps You Focused. Your *"why"* grounds you and keeps you on track. By staying connected with your values, you stay focused on what's important. Tap into the vision for your life when it's time to make decisions.

A clear '*Why*' helps you attract more into Your Life. After you've **become your own why**, you'll find that you are able to attract abundance.

Journaling

Transformation rarely happens overnight. Begin by setting aside time for reflection — journaling your thoughts, feelings, prayers, dreams, and even your uncertainties. In each moment of stillness, you may uncover a spark of inspiration that leads to profound change.

Take pride in your journey. Remember, this phase isn't about erasing the past but about integrating all that you are now, into a renewed sense of purpose.

Imagine seeing what you wrote in your journal today, to serve as evidence in the future of what you achieved, this would be so rewarding.

Explore different experiences

Navigating this new landscape does not have to be a solitary journey. Reach out to friends, join groups, or find a mentor who resonates with your aspirations. Sharing your journey with others can offer fresh perspectives, accountability, and a deep sense of belonging. In a community of like-minded individuals, you'll find that many are also discovering their **Next Best You**.

The shared experiences of empty nesters create a tapestry of stories — stories of resilience, reinvention, and unyielding hope. Celebrate these connections as you build a network of support that nurtures your spirit and fuels your journey.

Lighting Your Inner Flame

At the heart of this transformation is the realization that your purpose has always been within you. **Becoming your own why** is about reclaiming that inner light and letting it guide you forward. It's a journey of self-compassion, curiosity, and bold steps into the unknown.

In moments of self-doubt, remember that the strength which raised your amazing children is the same strength that can lift the amazing you, into a future of endless possibilities. Every challenge is an opportunity for growth, and every moment of reflection is a chance to tune into your deepest passions.

Ways to Become Your Own Why:

1. *Reconnect with Your Passions* – Revisit old hobbies, explore new interests, and invest in activities that bring you joy.

2. *Prioritize Self-Care* – Focus on your mental, emotional, and physical well-being. Exercise, meditate, and engage in self-reflection.

3. *Set Personal Goals* – Whether it's learning a new skill, pursuing a career change, or traveling, give yourself goals that not only challenge you, but excite you too.

4. *Build a New Community* – Find support in groups, meet new friends, and surround yourself with people who inspire and uplift you.

5. *Embrace Continuous Learning* – Take classes, read books, and expand your knowledge in areas that interest you.

6. *Celebrate Small Wins* – Every step toward rediscovering yourself is valuable. Acknowledge and appreciate your progress, no matter how small.

7. *Give Yourself Permission to Dream* – Your future is still unwritten, and you have every right to create a fulfilling and meaningful life for yourself.

I started saying yes to new experiences with new people. I am traveling, both Chelsey and Austin have traveled internationally and now I am making it happen for me. I explored career opportunities that are now taking me International. I have invested in my well-being. And in the process, I've discovered something powerful: I was still needed — not just by my children, but Shelia needed Shelia.

Becoming my own why, meant recognizing that my value did not diminish when my children grew up. It meant understanding that I was worthy of a life filled with passion, purpose, and fulfillment beyond motherhood. My journey was not over; it was simply evolving.

Now, I wake up with a different kind of purpose — not one dictated by a schedule of swim and dance practices or school events, but one that is fueled by my own dreams and aspirations. I still love my children deeply, and I will always be their mother, but I am also my own person.

And that is enough.

Signs You Have Become Your Own Why:

1. *You Feel a Sense of Purpose Beyond Others* – You wake up excited about your own goals, rather than just focusing on others' needs.

2. *You No Longer Feel Lost in the Silence* – Instead of feeling empty, you embrace the quiet as an opportunity for self-reflection and personal growth.

3. *You Make Decisions Based on Your Desires* – You confidently prioritize your own happiness without guilt.

4. *You Feel Whole on Your Own* – Your identity is no longer solely tied to being a mother, but as an individual with dreams, passions, and ambitions.

5. *You Invest in Your Growth and Happiness* – Whether it's learning something new, traveling, or taking care of yourself, you make your personal fulfillment a priority.

6. *You Celebrate Your Own Wins* – You take pride in your own achievements, just as you did with your children's.

7. *You No Longer Seek External Validation* – Your self-worth comes from within, rather than needing approval from others.

8. *You Embrace Change with Openness* – You see life's transitions as opportunities to grow rather than obstacles.

9. *You Feel Inner Peace and Contentment* – You are at peace with where you are in life, recognizing that your value has never diminished.

10. *You Inspire Others by Simply Being Yourself* – Without trying, you become an example for other mothers navigating the same transition.

Conclusion: The Promise of a New Dawn

As you stand at the threshold of this new chapter of your life, embrace the journey with open arms. **The Next Best You** isn't a destination but a continuous evolution—a commitment to living authentically and courageously. In reclaiming your inner *"why"*, you are not only forging a path for your own renewal of life but also inspire others to embark on their transformative journeys.

Let this chapter be a reminder: the power to redefine your life lies within you. Embrace the freedom of the empty nest, celebrate every step of your journey, and know that your story of reinvention is only just beginning. Your inner flame, once dimmed by the demands of motherhood, is ready to blaze a trail toward a future filled with purpose, passion, and endless possibility.

To every mother standing at the crossroads of an empty nest, wondering what comes next—I want you to know this: You are still here. You still matter. And it is never too late to **become your own why**.

So, I ask you—what is one dream you've put on hold? Take one step toward it today.

DR. SHELIA EGGLESTON

ABOUT AUTHOR
Dr. Shelia Eggleston

Shelia Eggleston stands at the forefront of a new .... .era in personal and professional development. With her remarkable blend of strategic acumen, servant leadership, and unwavering commitment to helping others, she has carved a path that embodies the true essence of success and fulfillment.

As the Founder and CEO of S.E.E. (Shelia Eggleston Enterprises), Shelia has masterfully cultivated an enterprise that is more than just a business—it's a platform for transformation. With a focus on business mentoring and development. Shelia's expertise is centered around revenue multiplying, business life skills, and entrepreneurial success paths.

Shelia's journey towards becoming a beacon of inspiration has been fueled by an unquenchable thirst for knowledge, achievement, and a genuine desire to uplift her community. Armed with diverse degrees in vast vocations spanning marketing, global real estate, project management, product development and more, she has honed a multifaceted skill set that underpins her success.

For over two decades, Shelia has donned the mantle of a Servant-Leader across diverse realms, from faith-based initiatives to local and international business sectors. Currently, her strategic brilliance shines as she serves in the realm of business development for Integrity International Trade and Business Network (IITBN), a global powerhouse fostering sustainable economic growth and investment in Africa. This unwavering dedication was lauded as she stepped into the role of Chief Strategy Officer (CSO) for IITBN in August 2023. Shelia also serves as the CSO and International Advisor for the non-profit arm, HER EM-PACT International.

Shelia's leadership prowess is epitomized by her certifications in pivotal business disciplines, positioning her as a guiding light for aspiring business professionals. Shelia holds the Designation of CIPS (Certified International

Property Specialist) with the Real Estate Business Institute as a Global Realtor, reflects her versatility and mastery.

Shelia is the Founder and CEO of Opport**unity** Africa. At Opport**unity** Africa, we believe in a world where opportunity is shared—not separated by geography, income, or history. The name reflects our mission: to unite African entrepreneurs with diaspora and global investors. We are launching a movement rooted in unity— where capital becomes a connector, entrepreneurship becomes empowerment, and Africans at home and abroad invest in each other's success.

However, beyond her professional achievements, Shelia's heart is firmly rooted in her community and her cherished circle of family and friends. A world changer with a compassionate soul, she embodies the true essence of a humanitarian.

In Dr. Shelia Eggleston, we find not just a leader, but a trailblazer whose journey has been fueled by faith, talent, and the unyielding belief that the future holds boundless opportunities. As she continues to navigate the realms of entrepreneurship, leadership, and humanity, Shelia remains an exemplary figure—an embodiment of what is achievable when one's faith converges with their innate gifts and the vast doors of opportunity swing wide open.

Connect with Dr. Shelia
shelia@sheliaeggleston.com

REINVENTING THE BEST, YOU!
By Dr. Deborah Allen

L et's go and be fiercely ignited. In this grand journey of reinventing the best you, you've come to a pivotal juncture. You've already mustered the courage to embark on this path, and now, as you move forward, greatness calls out to you. You see, my friend, it's time to evolve into the greatest version of yourself. Remember, nothing in life remains static, and neither should you. Time, the relentless force that it is, brings change and growth to our lives and to the world. It's your moment to change, to develop gradually from a simpler form to a more complex one – to evolve.

Oh yes! Reinventing you will call for you to evolve! Emerge into the greatest version of you for you and the nation you are called to. Deep within you, there's a fierce spirit embedded in your core. This fierceness is your ally, your source of strength as you navigate the inner transformation required for this evolution. Just like a superhero, you have the incredible ability to evolve, to go through life's challenges and shifts without being defeated. In fact, you're not just motivated; you're laser-focused on victory. To truly evolve, maturity and a cleansing of your mind are mandatory steps. It's time to bid farewell to the mindset of a child and welcome the victorious adult within you. Strengthen your mind, your thoughts, your dreams, and your goals. Your mind must rise to the challenge of handling your growth.

Clarity has become your guide, helping you discern the high stakes involved if you choose to remain where you are. The past is a place you can't reside in, dwell on, or grieve over. Your gaze is firmly fixed on the horizon of your future, and you're moving in for the kill, zeroing in on your dreams with tunnel vision. This fierce determination, embedded within your core, propels you forward. You're not merely chasing your destiny; you're stalking it, with unwavering resolve. Your hard work will be the tool you use to pay off your debts and bills. You're on the path to leaving a lasting legacy, for your children, your church, charities, and the next generation. Your impact will extend far beyond your community, reaching a national, global, and even international scale. You've ignited a fierce movement, and its transformative flow is inspiring countless others around you. You've become a connector of destinies, changing lives in the process. You are a vital part of a larger plan, a source of inspiration and change. You're not just a participant; you're the door through which greatness and transformative events will pass. This is the beginning of a worldwide pandemic of power and purpose.

VICTORIOUS TRANSFORMATION

You, my friend, are a dynamic force. Your empowerment is changing the very dynamics of the world around you. People look to you for guidance, and this means you must stand firm in your beliefs and your mission. Many are looking to follow your lead, and you're setting an example for your community, children, coworkers, and countless others. You're not dwelling in victimhood or succumbing to adversity. You're relentless in your pursuit of change, growth, and fulfilling your calling. You are free to evolve, to grow, and to become the person you were meant to be. You're in the process of becoming the new and improved version of yourself. We come from diverse backgrounds – different nationalities, cultures, colors, and creeds – but we need each other to thrive and to be strong. It's your responsibility to show and teach the youth to be independent, to build their lives with purpose.

There's no doubt about it; you can have what you want, and you have the power to speak your dreams and goals into existence. Be vocal about bringing forth your vision. You are complete and whole in yourself; you don't need anyone to complete you. Singleness isn't a hindrance; it's an opportunity to birth your purpose.

Now, it's time to break free from that dead-end job that's been draining you, stifling your creativity, and wearing you out. The stability of keeping that job is no longer guaranteed. The world is changing, and it's time to seize new opportunities, whether it's starting that business you've always dreamed of or pursuing the promotions you've had your eye on. You've got what it takes, and your winning season has arrived. The harvest is here, and everything you've believed, prayed for, hoped for, and sought is right in front of you. All you have to do is pursue, and you will not only recover what you've lost but conquer new territories. For you are great, wise, powerful, and fiercely determined. You are a survivor, celebrating the wins in your life, from childbirth to marriage, from jobs to business endeavors, from ministry to the challenges of aging. You've not only survived; you've evolved. You are not a loser. Losing is not in your DNA. Everything that has tried to stand in your way, to halt your progress, has not and will not succeed. The dreams that have been stirring within you, along with the business ventures waiting to be born, are now ready to come to life. You've entered the perfect moment, and you are the perfect creation to make it happen. You will get it done. Be free, be inspired, and never let defeat gain a foothold in your life. Reinvent the best you because within you lies a fierce beauty, an epic story, and a resilience born of life's trials.

The Fierce System:

1. **F** – Find yourself…Find your true self and be true to your own voice, dreams and goals.

2. **I** – Indeed be independent... Indeed be independent for you are the difference maker in your life and the entire world.
3. **E**- Evaluate your life & story... Evaluate your story and life from clear eyes and not them eyes of your past and unlearned you.
4. **R** – Realize you make the difference... Realize life is better because you are here and have purpose to fulfill.
5. **C** – Create opportunity through purpose... Create opportunity through purpose the gift in your hand that will bring you before great men and allow you to make wealth.
6. **E** – Evolve into the greatest version of you... Evolve into the greatest version of you that the process of time has allowed you to become who you was born to be.

The FIERCE System was created because of the darkest years of my life. I had to decide to either quit, wallow in pity or get back up again and win. It does not matter where you start but it matters where your mindset is. I had to first deal with the battle of my own mindset and limitations before I could finally see clear. The greatest thing I did was to dream again. Not only that I started fantasying about long ago visions that I killed in my mind as impossible. Then I meditated and got strategy which became, The FIERCE System. As I applied every letter and step mighty things began to take place. What I start believing for, looking for was already seeking me and that was destiny. Take the limits off your eyes and mind. That way you could truly see the brilliance of your life. It will enlarge your territories and set you free to be fiercely and unapologetically you!

"When walking in purpose, fiercely walk in authority!" ~ *Apostle Dr. Deborah Allen*

*******I have a gift for you:
https://deborahallen.groovepages.com/free/index *******

DR. DEBORAH ALLEN SIGNATURE PROGRAM LINK
https://sites.google.com/view/executive-firce-coaching/home

ACKNOWLEDGMENTS

Writing will forever be a great testament of the movement that being an author has brought into my life and the lives of the masses on a global scale. I'm grateful for all the support and love that has been so graciously shown to me throughout the years. Kudos and a special thanks to Fierce Tv (viewers) and The Fierce, Ignition & Activation Show/Podcast (listeners). Please know I am forever grateful!

I serve in ministry with a mighty man of valor, Apostle Dr. Glen Allen Sr, who has embraced the fierceness in me. **Lighthouse Apostolic Ministries of God Church** *"The House of The Prophets"* a sincere thank you for always being a place of advancement, change, purpose, vision, love even dreams.

Wondrously, I have had six children, but I'm the mother of nine. Our children have been a blessing to my very existence. I'm so awed by my support from family, friends, and clients. All your love has been priceless. You have been the *"why"* inside of me!

Finally, I want to express a heartfelt thanks to my Lord, Jesus for calling me to be yours!

Apostle Dr. Deborah Allen

ABOUT AUTHOR
Dr. Deborah Allen

Finding one's *inner voice,* can be a liberating, awe-inspiring, and transformational experience. Fashioned to help the masses find their *"fierce"*; is the dynamic professional, Deborah Allen.

Deborah Allen is a 45X best-selling & 22X international best-selling author, speaker, certified life-coach, cleric, and CEO and creative founder of "The Fierce System;" a multifaceted liaison specialty, centered around helping women to both, find and develop, their voice. Having been trained by world-renowned NSA motivational speaker, Mr. Les Brown, Deborah understands the importance of strategy, development, and credible mentorship; traits she seamlessly translates, to her growing clientele.

Deborah's mantra is simple:
Her one and only goal is to motivate clients; helping them to create the life, they were meant to live.

Refusing mediocrity on all fronts, Deborah has trailblazed a credible path for those she serves. She has served as Senior Pastor of Lighthouse Apostolic Ministries of God Church, for the last 24 years; and is the Executive Director of the nonprofit organization, L.A.M. Ministries, Inc.

Matching servant leadership with an incredible respect for higher learning, Deborah is a Certified Life Coach; and is a member of the National Speaker Association Speaker (NSA) and a Black Speakers Network (BSN) Speaker. Her conglomerate The Fierce System, is comprised of many platforms, including: Fierce TV, Radio, and blog; as well as Fierce Voices of Destiny Program; where she mentors, develops, and creates strategic alignment between clients, and their true life's calling. She is the Visionary and CEO of Igniting The Flame Publishing, Visionary Coaching & Consulting Group LLC and Deborah Allen Enterprise. Dr. Deborah graduated October 29,2022 with her Dr. of Philosophy and Christian Leadership from Cornerstone Christian University in Atlanta, Ga.

Deborah proudly attests that women are at the heartbeat of all she does, and that it is her desire to see them be strong, fierce, and know, that they can truly achieve their dreams, and walk in purpose. When she is not out helping women to come alive, rebuild, shift and find themselves again; Deborah is a valued asset to her communal body, and a loving member of her family and friendship circles.

Dr. Deborah Allen. Energizer. Organizer. Servant Leader

Connect with Apostle Dr. Deborah Allen

www.deborahallenfierce.com

www.ignitingtheflamepublishing.com

Email: deborahallenfierce@gmail.com

Links:
Facebook: https://www.facebook.com/deborahallenfierce

Instagram: https://www.instagram.com/deborahallenfierce/

Twitter: https://twitter.com/deborahallenfie
YouTube: https://www.youtube.com/channel/UCTOf0igcAxl VaneH2ZOo_Zg
2nd Website: https://deborahallenspeaker.com/

STEPPING INTO YOUR FUTURE SELF

By Dr. Jodie Solberg

"People often say that this or that person has not yet found himself. But the self is not something one finds; it is something one creates." –Thomas Szasz

Who you were yesterday does not determine who you will become tomorrow. You are not defined by your past or your circumstances. You have the power of choice, and that power allows you to become the next best version of yourself every day. It certainly takes intention and consistent action, but nothing is predetermined. You get to create your future by waking up each day and choosing to step into it.

Throughout life, there are many transitions. We reinvent ourselves repeatedly with each new season. Growing up, I was shy, quiet, reserved, and would never have been described as outgoing. But I loved people and had many friends and a few very close ones. I got good grades and always knew I would go to college and be a therapist to help people. I knew who I wanted to become. But it was a long process to get there. I got my first two degrees in Psychology and Sociology because I wanted to understand and help people on an individual level and how they interacted in relationships with one another.

When I started my internships, I was immediately thrust into the world of families in crisis, supervising visits for severe abuse cases to give custody recommendations to social workers and the courts and teaching parenting training classes. I had to step into who I wanted to become for so many years. I was younger than most of the parents and looked even younger than I was, so I had to overcome my own insecurities about my age, develop confidence in my knowledge and abilities, and be assertive.

My next life transition came in the form of becoming a business owner. While in graduate school, I decided to start my entrepreneurial journey by consulting and coaching women in business to help pay off my mountain of student loans. Suddenly, I was stepping into a new role of teaching people about professional image, how to present themselves in business, and how to build client bases and do marketing. All while doing it myself.

While I do have entrepreneurship in my family, it was my first venture into the world of business, and I was terrified of public speaking. But I chose to step into who I wanted to become. Between networking, speaking in front of groups for my business, and having all my therapy sessions videotaped and reviewed in a boardroom each week for school, over the years, I expanded my comfort zone and became the confident speaker I am today.

Over the years, those groups got larger, and my comfort zone grew along with them. I remember going to events with speakers with huge followings, such as Tony Robbins, and thinking I could never see myself on stage like that. But as I continued to step into the role of business leader, transformational speaker, and eventually international best-selling author, I can now say that I have spoken on many stages with incredible mentors I used to only watch from the crowd, such as Les Brown, and I have even co-authored with him! If you had told me that fact decades ago, I never would have believed you. But with each new season, I evolved, first as a therapist and coach, then as a military wife and a homeowner, and from a city dweller to living in a small town in the foothills of the mountains. I have achieved financial success in my career while also experiencing chronic burnout and then made the conscious decision to think, act, and be different to heal from within and recreate my success sustainably so that it supports my health and well-being while caring for others. I evolved over time into who I am today as an individual, as a mental wellness professional, as a success coach and hypnotherapist in private practice, and as a speaker and author. Every step has gotten me closer to who I was truly meant to become.

Each time I transitioned, I would step into my future self, embodying what I had only previously aspired to be, and choose to engage in the process of becoming the next best version of myself. Chances are, you have gone through many incarnations of yourself as well. We all go from childhood to adolescence to adulthood, moving from being a student to joining the workforce. Since then, perhaps you have become a partner, a spouse, a parent, an empty nester, or a caregiver. You may have reinvented yourself by changing careers after being laid off or retiring and starting a new chapter. And each time you stepped into your future self. Remember back to one of those times when it was the first day you chose to become a whole new you, such as the first day of a new job or when you got married or became a parent.

I'm here to show you that you can choose to make a change at any time. You don't have to wait for life to present a transition to you. Regardless of who you were yesterday, you have the power of choice, and right now, you can choose to step into your future self. All it takes is figuring out who that next version of you will be and then taking that first step in and forward.

While we may not have control over everything that happens to us, we can choose our beliefs, thoughts, behaviors, and the lens through which we view the world and how we choose to respond to the things that happen in our lives. Our current actions shape our future, so visualizing who we want to become, our future self, and taking intentional steps toward our goals and that vision is key.

The first step in creating your vision for your future self is to understand that while your past doesn't define you, it is important to learn from it. You can choose to reflect, taking all the lessons you have learned and wisdom you have gained with you moving forward, and then leave the rest behind you. The self-doubt and insecurities, the comfort zones you were stuck in, and the habits and patterns that no longer serve you can all be released. Take the time to look at how everything you have been through so far in life has shaped your character, what those experiences gave you the gift of allowing you to learn from them, and how they have made you stronger, wiser, and better.

The next step is to get to know you deep down inside. Without judgment or trying to be anyone else, get to know yourself, your values, priorities, strengths, likes and dislikes, and how your brain works. And begin to work with it rather than constantly fighting against yourself and trying to be like someone else. Let go of the constant comparison, the shoulds, the pressures, and expectations. Identifying your values and priorities can help you make decisions that align with your future self because your future self is already inside of you, waiting to be released.

When we try to be something other than our true selves, we become out of alignment and experience a lack of fulfillment, passion, purpose, and energy. So, it's time to get to know yourself, accept and acknowledge yourself, and start asking the tough questions. What has been keeping you stuck in the same old patterns, preventing you from moving forward? How have you been benefiting from staying the same? And how has staying the same been detrimental to your life? What habits or patterns need to change for you to grow? What boundaries do you need to set with yourself and others to move forward? What areas are you naturally strong in, and how can you embrace those strengths more in your life? What needs to be released from the past to become the next best version of yourself? The answers may surprise you, but they will be invaluable in realizing how you have been holding yourself back from becoming your own best version of yourself.

Once you have gotten clear about where you are now, it's time to explore who your future self is going to be. Sit down with a journal and just let it all flow, writing down everything you can imagine your ideal life to be. Consider all aspects of the experience of your future self-such as your career, relationships, personal growth, physical health, thought processes, energy, how you will dress and carry yourself, and where you will live. No detail is too small. Imagine yourself interacting with others, what you are saying, and how you impact their lives. Remember when creating the story of your future self that it is truly about yourself and no one else. Allow your inner wisdom to guide you, as the answers to who you are becoming are already inside of you. As business magnate Steve Jobs once said, *"Have the courage to follow your heart and intuition. They somehow already know what you truly want to become. Everything else is secondary."*

After you have written the story of your future self, it's time to create the vision of the next best version of you and learn to step into that vision. Close your eyes and imagine your future self is standing in front of you. How will you feel when you realize your goals and that story is your own reality? Now, continue to dive deeper into what matters to you in creating this future for yourself. What will it really mean to you to reach that goal? How will becoming your future self positively impact your life and the lives of others? Now, imagine stepping into that vision so that you feel as if you are already there. Feel those good feelings, and the energy shift in who you have become. Once you have this new perspective, describe it in as much detail as possible. Does this vision of yourself feel more in alignment with who you were created to be? How will that experience influence your thoughts, feelings, and behaviors from this point in the present moment moving forward?

One of the things that may come up for you when doing this exercise and answering these questions is resistance. Something deep inside of you may be scared or protective of you, trying to keep you in the comfort zone of what you already know. These feelings likely come from limiting beliefs such as fear of failure, uncertainty, or unworthiness. Notice any negative self-talk that comes up for you when you envision your future self and write it down. Then, say them aloud to yourself. Would you ever say those things to anyone else who shared their dreams with you? And if someone you cared about said those negative things about themselves, what compassionate words would you say back to them in response? It's human nature to be our own worst critics, so this will teach you to have self-compassion and to identify the limiting beliefs you have that have been holding you back from moving toward that vision.

What are more supportive beliefs that can help you to take steps forward? Create affirming statements to back up those new beliefs, starting with the words I am. One example would be, *"I am learning/growing/getting closer to becoming the very best version of myself every day."* Insert into that sentence whatever you are working towards in your vision. This will enlist your subconscious mind in helping you to take steps toward your vision rather than blocking you at every turn.

The next step in becoming your future self is setting goals that will create momentum to get you closer to the vision you created and then taking aligned action. That means making choices that reflect your values and priorities and breaking your goals down into small, manageable steps. When you stay consistent and growth-oriented, consistently repeating those I am affirming statements, and recognize yourself for each step along the way, you will see momentum begin to build. Political ethicist Mahatma Ghandi said that *"Your future depends on what you do today."*

Each day, as you take aligned action, you make positive changes and become your best self. That isn't to say that there won't ever be obstacles. Acknowledge that setbacks are inevitable and accept them as a natural part of the journey on the path to your future self. They are quite literally how you will gain the required knowledge and wisdom along the way.

So, look at those setbacks as an opportunity to learn where to course correct and embrace them for the milestones in your journey toward your future vision that they are. Be flexible, and make sure to reflect on your progress regularly. Celebrate all of the little milestones and stay motivated by keeping your vision in front of you and connecting to it daily. Each day, when you wake up, choose to be intentional about moving forward toward your future self. Close your eyes, revisit your vision, and step into those feelings once again. *"A growth mindset is the belief you can develop abilities."* This is a quote from psychologist Carol Dweck, whose work focuses on mindset and motivation. Believe that you can grow, create positive change, and evolve into who you are becoming. That person is already inside of you; all you must do is allow yourself to be that version of yourself.

Each one of us is on a continuous journey of growth and discovery in our lives. And every day you wake up, you are stepping into who you are becoming. It's up to you to choose who that will be. As a hypnotherapist, I guide my clients through the journey I just described to you of stepping into their future selves to actively create their next best version of themselves. All the answers are already inside of them; I simply facilitate the finding of those answers by teaching them to tap into their inner wisdom and potential to become who they want to create. Please know that you don't have to do it alone. I offer support and guidance in identifying, healing, and releasing the root cause of whatever has been holding you back and then building the vision of who you are becoming moving forward. Reach out for the support you need to create the life you want for yourself. And every day when you wake up, remember as you step out of bed to step into your future self. Do that consistently and intentionally, and the next thing you know, that future self will be the present you.

ABOUT AUTHOR

Dr. Jodie Solberg

Jodie Solberg is a Mental Wellness and Success Coach and Certified Master Hypnotherapist. She is also a Transformational Speaker and International Best-Selling Author with a Doctorate in Christian Counseling. Jodie loves working with purpose-driven individuals who are on a mission to live in alignment with their passion and values to create real and lasting change in their lives and the world around them. She helps them tap into the power of their inner wisdom to gain the clarity and confidence they need to Level Up and achieve their personal and professional goals.

Jodie has been working therapeutically and as a coach for over 20 years, with an educational background in both Social and Clinical Psychology. Her transformative programs build self-esteem and confidence and increase her clients' focus, strength, resilience, and emotional intelligence. Jodie also teaches clients the importance of prioritizing self-care and guides them in healing from past trauma to avoid burnout, cultivate mental wellness, and adopt a growth mindset to effect positive change from within.

Founding Psyched Up Success in 2019, Jodie fulfilled a long-standing dream of having her own private mental wellness practice, working virtually with clients worldwide. Jodie's greatest joy and purpose is helping others find their voice, become their best selves, create a life they love, and pass those lessons on to the next generation. In addition to her professional fulfillment, she is a great contributor to her community, with a long history of volunteerism. Jodie has always been a believer in creating work-life harmony, so she also enjoys spending time outdoors and traveling with her family in search of great food, music, and culture.

Connect with Dr. Jodie

jodie@psychedupsuccess.com
www.psychedupsuccess.com
Instagram @psyched_up_success
Facebook at @psychedupsucces

BEYOND THE VEIL OF GRIEF:

DISCOVERING PURPOSE THROUGH LOSS

By Alanna Turtle

G rief is a complex and deeply personal journey, weaving its way through the rich fabric of our lives. Within its intricate tapestry, it carries the potential for impactful change, leaving threads of sorrow, longing, and seeds for evolution. Profound experiences of loss and healing have marked my journey – each a testament to the tenacity of the human spirit and the power of love to transcend even the darkest nights. I have learned that healing is not a destination but a path, that when traversed with courage and compassion, can metamorphosize into a transformative blend of experiences.

My journey began long before the final farewell. In my youthful innocence, I firmly believed that every child naturally nurtured a meaningful and unyielding connection with their mothers. As my consciousness expanded and my comprehension of relationships matured, it became apparent that this assumption did not apply universally. I was fortunate to have had an unbreakable bond with my mother. One that fueled the genesis of my transformation and continues to drive my evolutionary progress.

I was ignited when my mother made the courageous decision to embark on the challenging path of divorce. It was a choice weighed down by years of hurt, disappointment, and shattered expectations. For too long, she clung to the belief that her relationship with my father should endure despite cracks that had formed beneath the surface. With each passing day, the weight of unfulfilled promises grew heavier until finally, with the unwavering support of her three daughters, she armed herself with the courage to break free from the cycle of pain and disillusionment. She valiantly confronted the aftermath of familial shock and discord, assuming command of her destiny in an ethnical culture that often cast a disappointing eye on such assertive choices.

In supporting her through this decision, I witnessed the alchemy gained from the power of self-love and self-preservation. I experienced the wave of liberation as she broke herself free from the chains of despair. During the tumult of the divorce, I became my mother's steadfast companion and together, we weathered the tempest of emotions. Through the darkness of uncertainty, we forged a fortified bond that transcended the confines of unsupportive familial ties. Both of us emerged more resilient.

The echoes of divorce were still resonating and had yet to fade into the background when, immediately after losing my grandmother, a new challenge emerged on the horizon. Life presented my mother with an insidious adversary – an unrelenting battle with heart disease. A struggle that she stood bold-faced and in defiance of succumbing to until its presence could no longer be ignored.

She surprisingly accepted the proposed medical intervention despite her initial and steadfast vow to surrender to the natural order. Perhaps she had felt inspired to intertwine herself more meaningfully with her children or thought to enjoy the newfound liberation post-divorce offered. Nevertheless, she met the call of her heart with an inspiring fortitude. She forged ahead daily, exuding warmth and laughter, effortlessly comforting those around her as her surgery date approached. Forever ingrained is the sight of her giggling and storytelling as they whisked her away on the fateful morning.

Shock soon followed, for her mental and emotional endurance was not rewarded with any leniency. We stood shoulder to shoulder for the next ten arduous years, confronting the repercussions of that failed hospital procedure. Kevin, my unwavering husband, was a pillar of strength for both of us during those trying times, unswerving even while walking the turbulent path of this journey with us. Together, we witnessed the mere will of her spirit, refusing to yield to despair, as it constantly flickered with optimism that she would miraculously recover.

She was a shining example that when hope seemed elusive, determination was the torch with which to forge ahead. I unconsciously chose to serve as a conduit for the essence through which she experienced life—thriving and embodying joy and determination, primarily for her, resolute in my promise to never leave her side and to continuously provide inspiration and motivation for her to heal. In her declining state of health, even when anger replaced possibility, a delusion took root within me, fostering the belief that she would persist indefinitely in her ailing condition. This mirage shattered when notwithstanding her best efforts, my mother's light faded into eternity.

The pain of her loss was a tidal wave that threatened to engulf me, leaving me gasping for breath. The grief that followed was an abyss, consuming me whole and leaving me adrift and drowning in a sea of sorrow. Kevin was one of the sole reasons that each day after her death, I chose to breathe, to endure, and to remember that his love possessed the strength to carry me through the shadowed hours of grieving.

On the earthly plane, I had lost not only a mother but a cheerleader, a confidant, and what felt like a piece of my soul.

This overwhelming sadness was a burden so heavy that one day, as I dragged myself up onto my shaky legs, I realized that I had forgotten who I even was—my identity swept away with every tear I had shed. The darkness in which I had chosen to entrench myself bubbled up a sudden awareness that the sword driving the anguish even deeper was a petrifying fear disguised as sadness.

It became starkly apparent that my role as a caretaker for my mother had quietly become the cornerstone of my identity, and this fear now drove the constant waves of debilitating sorrow. For years, I had navigated the familiar rhythms of worry and found a satiable comfort in the frustration of caring for her needs. With her departure, what felt like an insurmountable void emerged, leaving me adrift in the vast expanse of uncertainty. An overwhelming sense of self-devastation engulfed me.

Many expected my behaviour to exhibit that of a champion. It was assumed that I would provide consolation to those in my surroundings by burying myself in the routine of work and concealing my grief with a smile. Alternatively, I found myself grappling with an overwhelming sense of dissatisfaction with my current reality. Despite being surrounded by safety, fortune, and the loving embrace of a supportive husband, I felt trapped in a cycle of repetition, devoid of purpose or meaning. It was as if the very essence of my identity had become severed from the moorings of familiarity and routine.

Amidst the turmoil of this uncertainty, a glimmer of possibility began to germinate in the form of a forlorn prayer. As I gazed into the mirror one morning, I remember uttering a heartfelt plea for grace and guidance to illuminate the passage out of my blinding despair. There had to be a more extraordinary life beyond the depths of this melancholy. Certainly, I could honour the memory of my beloved mother in a more enlightened way, and I pleaded to whomever unseen that I conjure the capability to express my profound appreciation for my husband's undying support, especially as he grappled with his own sense of loss.

The waves of grief eventually morphed into a constant tide of fear. They washed over me with the realization that I was adrift in uncharted waters - the tides slowly uncovering a whisper of change and gently ushering me toward a new chapter. After a prolonged drowning in despondency, the call to shed the cocoon of complacency and release this petrification began to radiate subtle ripples and nudges. I sensed a way forward yet could not discern how to break free. It was while I was riding these swells that a furry companion entered my life, Tizer, a puppy whose troubled soul mirrored my entrenched pain and frustration.

Through his eyes, I saw a reflection of my struggles, a silent reminder of the journey ahead. His deportment and physical health caused me to doubt my ability to be his human caretaker. My instincts, although dulled, kept gently nudging me that he was a catalyst meant to intersect my monotony and interrupt my state of mourning. In my determination to help him - and myself – to heal, find peace and a grounded sense of self, I found delight in exploring traditional training methods and alternative healing modalities. Tizer gifted me with the perspective that he was not giving me a hard time but that he was having a hard time. Not a sensation unknown to me.

I delved into every avenue I could uncover to understand the correlation of health and its elusive connection to behaviour. I was determined to provide well-being to an animal overwhelmed by the world around him. During this educational undertaking I unearthed my calling to be a healing practitioner and an energy intuitive – a path that resonated deep within my soul – and soon, gaps lying unfulfilled started shining with the missing light I had not known I had buried or forgotten, until the passing of my mother. Through developing a meditation practice, attuning to reiki, and following intuitive nudges, I restored my shattered heart, finding passionate direction.

This beautiful soul aligned me with the most glorious truth – that we are all energy and that embodying love is our birthright. All life presents us with opportunities to satisfy that pursuit. An actuality that my devoted husband, Kevin, had desired me to realize during my months of anguish. Tizer modelled my own needs, and by Intending to help an animal yearning to find balance, I found myself journeying along the intricate pathways of personal growth.

While navigating the maze of personal development, I welcomed my role as a channel for healing energies and intuitive insights. Through dedicated study, practice, and introspection, I uncovered the boundless potential of healing energy to permeate every facet of our existence. I was fortunate to align with remarkable mentors who nurtured and amplified my intuitive development. Their guidance and encouragement persistently empowered me to embody my calling with clarity and conviction.

Pivotal moments transpired when, through intuitive discernment, I gained a deeper understanding of the unique needs of my animals and those who sought my care. With empathic precision, cognizant attunement, and compassion as my guides, each session has become a sacred exchange of energy, unravelling the knots of pain and promoting rejuvenation and harmony. Radiance restored, igniting anew in its rightful place.

My odyssey from the depths of feeling forfeit to the empowering of others to recognize and embody their inherent wholeness, epitomizes the qualities that can be birthed from seeking clarity and inner peace. Through the crucible of grief, I excavated my inner fortitude and the limitless potential of the human heart to mend - because it is never actually broken. In the grand mosaic created by the illusion of feeling shattered, reflections of possibility and growth can manifest unexpected sources of atonement.

These opportunities can present themselves through the loss of a cherished one, the commitment of a devoted husband, or the distress of a troubled canine - all of which offered me the ability to cultivate and nurture unconditional love and to appreciate the significance that every event unfolds for our ultimate benefit. Even those bereft with pain. Especially those overflowing with excitement.

I found renewed meaning and connection by answering the call to serve others and their precious animals. Bereavement transmuted into the realization that we all can choose an effortless course through conscious choice and unattached inquiry. Each day, know that you can alchemize your thoughts from negativity, entrapment, and feeling adrift into enlightenment, understanding of purpose, and improved health. The polarity of emotion we experience is the stimulus to seek improvement and refine our thoughts. Be a source of inspiration and empowerment for those around you. Keep shining your light, even if it be a mere flicker, for it can illuminate even the darkest passage.

If you have an innate longing to achieve a sense of balance, relaxation or overall well-being or seek to improve your relationship with your beloved animals, contact me for a consultation or healing session at alanna@alannaturtle.com.

The road forged carves the ways for others to keep going, keep growing, and keep glowing.

ABOUT AUTHOR

Alanna Turtle

In the tapestry of life, where each thread holds healing potential, Alanna Turtle shines brightly with a healing gift that transcends the ordinary. As the founder of Turtle Touch, a center for healing, she melds the ancient practice of Reiki with the melodic principles of music and the crystalline energies of the earth into a sanctuary where spirits are uplifted, and hearts find renewal. This harmonious blend paves the way for her illustrious journey, beginning with a solid Music Performance foundation.

Her expertise is further enriched by her studies in Angel Card Mastery and Crystal Energy Guide, reflecting a commitment to embracing a wide range of healing modalities. This comprehensive approach not only defines her unique practice but also elevates it to unparalleled dimensions. Turtle Touch, Alanna's brainchild, embodies her vision to restore and strengthen the spiritual connection between the divine source and individuals. Her mission is clear and profound: to light the way for souls to discover their own brilliance, to foster growth, and to illuminate the path for others on their journey to enlightenment.

Alanna's healing touch transcends physical boundaries, extending her compassion and expertise across the globe through virtual sessions and offering profound in-person encounters. With a special affinity for canines, her holistic approach embraces not just humans but the entire animal realm, setting Turtle Touch apart as a haven for all seeking solace, renewal, and transformative healing. This inclusive and adaptable method ensures that anyone, anywhere, can benefit from her unique blend of healing energies, fostering connections and support on their journey towards wellness.

Driven by a deep desire to expand her intuitive gifts to their fullest potential, Alanna aspires to uplift humanity and the animal kingdom alike. Inspired by her supportive husband Kevin, her beloved cat Miami, and her dog Tizer — who sparked her transformative journey — and the teachings of spiritual leaders like Kyle Gray and Colette Baron-Reid, Alanna has crafted a path of service that merges her passions with her purpose.

"Keep going, keep growing, and keep glowing."

Connect with Alanna

alanna@alannaturtle.com

Instagram @alannaturtle

WHAT DOES THE NEXT BEST YOU LOOK LIKE?
By Dr. Donato Perricci

What do you think when you see the title of this book, Your Next Best You? Does it give you a reason to get Motivated? My hope is that it helps to motivate you, as it should show us that we can always do better and then help to show others the way also. I currently host a Podcast called **Get Motivated with Donato**. We should always strive to learn and grow as we live in this life we have. The journey is never over; we just change the direction of the destination. I have personally had some of those examples in my life.

One of my favorite quotes is from Ray Kroc, who said, *"When you are Green, you are Growing; and when you Ripe, you Rot!"* I heard this while working at McDonald's as a kid. Have you ever had something in your life like that? When you hear it or read it, it just gets inside of you. It motivates you and becomes part of your life. That is the purpose of this book and all the different chapters that are in it. I hope you will get something from this chapter that will be like that for you.

148

Please also take to heart all the other chapters from all the different people that are in this book. I strongly encourage and believe that we can learn from one another even if that person is vastly different. We all have a story to tell and need to be open to hearing from others who are brave enough to share. Maybe even reread the book from time to time to seek that encouragement that you need to get you inspired and motivated.

What are the things in life that shape you? That is kind of what this book and the title are all about. I am writing a book that should be out soon, if not already when you read this book, called Becoming the New You. It's interesting how close and similar these two books are. Maybe God has a message for people that He wants to get out. The great thing about a type of book like this is that you get many voices sharing their experiences. Whether or not you come from the same walk of life as some of the people in the book, you can learn something from their experiences. If we look hard enough, we all have something in common. I believe in having mentors from different walks of life so that we can gain different perspectives and broaden our understanding and minds.

Getting back to the things that shape you. Maybe you feel or think all is well. Perhaps that is true, but it doesn't mean you can't get better, learn something new, and share what you know. Many things shape us into who we are and/or who we may become. There are highs and lows that we all experience in life. Many of those things can shape us into the person we are. The problem is sometimes, we hang on to some of those bad things that have happened. We tend to build up walls and do other things that guard ourselves. We let those things impact us and then shape us into the person we are. It is time to tear down the walls and make a change. When you start to make a change and difference in your life, it will also improve your relationship with others and encourage them to become their Next Best selves.

Are those negative things still shaping you into the person you currently are? We are the only ones who can choose what we allow in and what we allow to stay in. That is a key part of all this. Everything that happens to us does shape us, but we can choose to learn from those experiences, put certain things behind us, and move forward, not letting the past govern what we do. The things that happen to us can be used to help others overcome the issues that they may be going through in life. We need to make the tests in our lives a testimony that can inspire others to get out of the issues they face.

As a pastor, I believe that God doesn't bring us to something without giving us the help to get through it. It may not seem like it at the time, though, as the circumstances may overwhelm us. Another thing that will help us is learning to change our mindset. When things happen to us, we tend to react to the issue and not take time to think about it and make a rational decision. We need to take a step back, try to think clearly, and give ourselves different options on how to solve the problem before acting and just flying off the rails. Sometimes, things need to be handled quickly, but if we learn how to condition ourselves with the right mindset, it will change how we process things. After we have gone through something, we are better equipped for the next time to better handle things that arise. This also has a lot to do with our attitude, which is a huge part of our mindset. Sometimes, our attitude can lead us into trouble if we are not thinking clearly. Keep in mind that sometimes we also experience things that may not seem like it at the time but are to our benefit.

Our mindset is also shaped by the things that happen to us and the choices or things we decide to make and follow. Our mindset is also part of our subconscious, and we may not know that we are doing something as it is programmed into us. This also affects the attitude that we have in life, whether we realize it or not. To start changing the things we do that are programmed into us, we need to change our conscious mind, flip that switch, and tell ourselves how it will be. This takes time and commitment to change. It has been said that it can take around 21 days to create a habit but twice as long to break it. If we are going to be able to change our mindset and reprogram ourselves, it is going to take time, so we cannot give up. To help with this process, I would encourage you to keep a journal that will help keep you on track and track your progress. Write down every day what it is that you want to accomplish and what you did accomplish. Do not get down on yourself if something doesn't happen immediately. Sometimes, the seeds that we plant take time to grow. Just keep focused and stay positive.

As part of this change, you need to be real with yourself. Ask yourself what it is that you want to change. What is it that you should change as this can be different? There may be different areas where you may want to change. Life, business, ministry, and other things that you are passionate about. What changes can you make to be the Next Best You? Then, you need to start making that change by flipping that switch and doing the positive things that will enforce that decision. You need to hear yourself saying it over and over. Though it may seem odd at the time, affirmation will help enforce that positive change you want. Be realistic, though, in what you want and speak out. We all would like to be a millionaire, but there are many steps to take to get there. Starting a business is maybe the first step to getting there. So, you can tell yourself I will start a business. Hopefully, you get the idea here. If you are too far out there when you speak it out, your mind will not believe you, and you may not get the results you are looking for. You can have the long-term goal of being a millionaire, but you need to speak out about the current things you need to change to get your mind on the right track. Sometimes, you need to take those baby steps before you can run.

You may be saying to yourself, but you don't know what I am going through. Or you don't understand what has happened to me. Maybe some of that is true. We all go through things in life, and I have had my fair share, as I am sure you have also. Once again, though the things we go through may shape us, we don't have to let them rule over us. When we take the time to look at ourselves and be honest with ourselves, we can start to put those things behind us and be that Next Best You. Keep in mind that we do this for ourselves. You don't need to do it for someone else. Don't let others dictate to you who you are going to be. It was one thing when we were growing up as children: our parents were trying to help us and shape us into good people. Now that we are older, we choose who we are going to be in life. You can ask those you trust for some insight or opinions; just be open to the truth. I think this can be a good thing if it is a person, you can trust and won't hurt you deliberately. You must be willing to hear what they say and take it to heart. I have done this at times to work the rough edges off in my own life.

Trust me, I know a thing or two about how hard life can be. One of the places I grew up in was Gary, Indiana. Let me tell you, it is one of the worst places to grow up. I could have let it dictate to me as to who I would be and be a street thug or something. Not to mention other things like my siblings being taken away when I was five years old and the sadness I faced with that. Or how about my mother deciding to leave when I was nine years old? There, again, are other hurts that I faced along the way as an adult. The point here is that though these things happen and may take time to heal properly; you don't need to let them guide you down the wrong path. If you are walking down the wrong way, the nice thing is you can change direction at any time. I have done this, and I know that you can, too. I have faced many challenges in life, and I am sure there will be more, but I have a foundation from which I can work. I hope this inspires you to build or improve your foundation. You can have and become anything you want to. I would have never thought I would have some of the things I do currently, and who knows what is still in store for me. The same can be true for your life. Do you want to have a Doctorate? I have one, why can't you? You know a little of what I have gone through. I am no better or different from you. You can do anything you set your mind to and have the right attitude in doing it.

Now is the time to take action with what you have just learned and will continue to learn throughout this book. If you do not have a journal, get one! Write down all your goals and dreams. Prioritize them, then focus on the top ones you want. Others may fade away, or some extras may come. Be deliberate in what you focus on and take the necessary steps to get you where you want to go. As we are complex beings with body, mind, and spirit, we must feed each part of who we are. Start a routine of 20 minutes doing something for your body every day. Then, 20 minutes to provide your mind with a topic of interest that may help you accomplish your goals. Also, make sure to take 20 minutes to feed your spirit and get lined up with God, as He will give you the strength to accomplish anything you want to do.

My prayer is that this chapter has touched you and will inspire you to keep learning and growing in life. If you need help, there is information in my bio to contact me, as I also provide coaching and mentoring.

ABOUT AUTHOR

Dr. Donato Perricci

Donato coaches and mentors people all around the world to become all that they can be. As in this chapter, you must start at the ground floor to move up and get higher. This goes for all walks of life and anything that you want to do. Donato does specialize in the business aspect of his coaching to get people to think outside of the box and get people to think about how things will also impact the future, not just the here and now.

Donato is a Pastor, Coach, Speaker, Author, Businessman, and so much more. Donato has been involved in many areas of ministry over the past 30 years and currently serves as the

Senior Pastor of Victory Celebration Family Church in the Twin Cities Metro area of Minnesota. Donato's desire is to impact people's lives with the Gospel and with everything he teaches. Donato's goal is to inspire, encourage, and build a person up to accomplish all their goals, dreams, and visions so they can be all God created for them to become.

Donato has been a leader in Corporate America for over 25 years. Donato has served in many different roles, most of which involve Technology. Donato has worked for many of the top Fortune 500 companies, handling many multi-million-dollar projects and the people involved. All these projects have many challenges, so Donato knows the stress of life that we all go through.

Donato grew up all around the Midwest, but he and his wife Nichol call Minnesota their home. They are parents and grandparents and love every minute of it. They own and operate a few businesses where they provide help to people who need websites, social media support, and much more.

Connect with Dr. Donato:

Website: https:\ \donatomotivates.com
Email: Donato@donatomotivates.com

THE FIRST STEP: RUNNING INTO INFINITE POSSIBILITY

By Dr. James Fomby

I t wasn't planned.

That's the part that still amazes me.

I wasn't standing on a track, preparing for a triumphant first run or basking in the anticipation of a long-awaited moment. I was in my home office, deeply engrossed in work, juggling tasks as the clock ticked toward my next meeting. I had ten minutes to spare before I needed to be back at my desk, and the horses needed to be fed.

So, I grabbed the feed bucket, headed toward the barn, and took off.

Halfway there, it hit me.

I wasn't walking. I was running.

For the first time in 35 years, I was running—legs moving freely, arms swinging, body working in perfect rhythm with something I hadn't felt in decades. The wind rushed against my face, my feet pounded the earth, and the barn ahead of me blurred through tears I hadn't realized were there.

When I reached the barn, I stopped, chest heaving, heart pounding—not from exertion, but from realization.

I fed the horses with trembling hands, my mind spinning, replaying the last 30 seconds over and over. I ran.

By the time I got back to the house, I leaned against the doorframe, staring at the AI-powered prosthetic leg strapped to me—a sleek, cutting-edge piece of technology that had quietly revolutionized my life.

But this moment wasn't just about the leg. It wasn't even just about running. This moment started years ago, when I hit my lowest point and made a decision that changed everything.

The Pandemic and the Weight of Inaction

Before the pandemic, I was already carrying extra weight. At 275 pounds, I wasn't where I wanted to be, but I was managing. I had my routines—walking into the office every day, moving throughout the day, staying somewhat active.

Then the world shut down.

Like so many others, I found myself working from home, cut off from the daily rhythms that had kept me moving. What I thought would be a temporary adjustment stretched into two and a half years. No more walking to meetings, no more steps around the office—just sitting at a desk at home, day after day.

The weight crept up slowly at first, and then all at once. I ballooned. My body became a reflection of everything I was holding onto—stress, uncertainty, and a growing sense of disconnection from who I wanted to be.

By the time I returned to a hybrid schedule, I wasn't just physically weighed down. I was emotionally stuck, unsure of how to break free.

The Prayer That Changed Everything

Everything changed the night I sat by my mother's bedside. She was at home, where she felt most comfortable, and her health was failing. The house was quiet, her strength fading, but her presence—steady, strong, and full of love—filled the room.

My sister had stepped out for a moment, leaving us alone. I sat beside her, holding her hand, her grip light but full of meaning.

"Mom," I said softly, my voice breaking. *"I am who I am today because of you."*

Her tired eyes met mine, and I felt the weight of everything she had given us—her sacrifices, her faith, her unconditional love.

"You've given me everything," I continued. *"Every good thing in me—every ounce of strength, resilience, and faith—I owe it all to*

you. You've shown me how to love without limits, how to keep going when life feels impossible, and how to trust God with everything."

We prayed together then, our hands clasped tightly. My voice cracked as I poured my heart out to God.

"Lord, thank you for this woman. Thank you for the life she's lived and the love she's poured into all of us. Thank you for the strength you've placed in her and the way she's shaped me into the person I am today."

And in that moment, I made a promise—to her and to God.

"Mom, I'm going to change. I'm going to take care of myself. I'm going to honor the life you've given me and live out the purpose God has placed in me."

Her hand squeezed mine gently, and though she didn't say much, her eyes said everything: I believe in you.

The Journey of Transformation

The promise I made that night became my turning point.

At 275 pounds, I was carrying the weight of years of neglect—neglecting my health, my body, and, in many ways, my own sense of purpose. But after that night, everything began to change.

Not all at once. Transformation rarely happens overnight. But slowly, steadily, I began to take small steps toward becoming the person I had promised to be.

I changed the way I ate, focused on movement, and gave myself grace for the journey. I lost 10 pounds, then 20, then 50. By the time I had lost 100 pounds, I felt like a completely different person—not just physically, but mentally and spiritually as well.

When I received the AI-powered prosthetic leg, it felt like a gift—an opportunity to take my transformation even further. But it wasn't just about the leg. The leg was ready long before I was. It wasn't until I had aligned my body, mind, and spirit with its capabilities that running became possible.

The First Run

That day at the barn wasn't just about running. It was about alignment.

The AI-powered prosthetic didn't carry me, and I didn't force it to follow. We moved together, in rhythm, in harmony. It responded to my every movement, not as something separate from me, but as an extension of who I was becoming.

As I ran, I felt a rhythm I hadn't felt in decades—a rhythm of freedom, possibility, and purpose. It wasn't just my body that was moving. It was my spirit, stepping into everything I had promised to my mother and to God.

The Dance: Partnering with the Right Tools

That run became a metaphor for everything I've learned since. It wasn't just about physical movement—it was about finding The Dance.

The Dance is about alignment—finding a rhythm with the tools and opportunities around you, letting them amplify your abilities and unlock your potential. Just like my AI-powered leg moved in harmony with my body, I began to see how other tools, like AI, could move in harmony with my mind, my creativity, and my purpose.

Run with AI

That's why I believe so deeply in this message: Run with AI.

Just as I discovered the freedom to run again after decades of believing I couldn't, I've seen people discover the freedom to create, solve problems, and embrace their potential with the help of AI.

It's not just about technology. It's about stepping into a rhythm that expands what's possible. It's about aligning yourself with the tools God has placed in your life and letting them amplify the gifts He's given you.

Your First Step

The most incredible moments in life are often the ones we don't plan—the ones that happen when we're simply moving forward, doing the work, showing up.

That's how it was for me on that day in the barn. I didn't set out to run. I didn't think I was ready. But when the moment came, I took the step—and it changed everything.

What about you? What's the step you've been waiting to take?

Here's how to get started:

Prompt Expanse

What's one challenge you're facing right now—something you've been stuck on or unsure how to approach? Ask AI to help you brainstorm solutions. Let it spark your imagination, and then refine the rhythm together.

Your step doesn't have to be perfect. It doesn't have to be planned. All it has to be is yours.

Let this be your starting line.

ABOUT AUTHOR
Dr. James Fomby

James Fomby is a pioneer at the intersection of faith, technology, and transformation. As a certified AI consultant, he is on a mission to empower ministries, entrepreneurs, and visionaries to embrace the infinite possibilities of artificial intelligence. With three decades of experience in technology, James has consistently turned challenges into breakthroughs—proving that resilience, innovation, and divine purpose can coexist in powerful ways.

His journey is nothing short of extraordinary. After decades of believing that running was no longer in his future, James experienced a life-altering moment with an AI-powered prosthetic leg—an experience that became the catalyst for his broader mission. His story is a testament to the power of alignment—mind, body, spirit, and technology working in harmony to unlock new potential.

James is the founder of **AIPostle**, a movement dedicated to equipping ministries with AI-driven tools that amplify their reach and impact. He leads with a heart for The Great Commission, ensuring that technology becomes a force for good in spreading faith and inspiration worldwide. His dynamic approach combines storytelling, hands-on coaching, and a visionary outlook that turns hesitation into action and uncertainty into confidence.

A sought-after speaker, trainer, and strategist, James is redefining what it means to Run with AI—not as a replacement for human creativity but as a partner in unlocking it. His work has inspired leaders across industries to embrace technology not as a threat, but as an extension of their God-given purpose.

With unwavering faith, an unshakable commitment to growth, and a deep understanding of AI's role in shaping the future, James Fomby is not just running—he's leading the way.

Connect with Dr. James

@james.fomby.2024

A DIFFERENT KIND OF VOICE

By Felicia Calcoate

MY name is Felicia Calcoate and I have been living without being able to express verbally my needs, my happiness, or my sorrow. I was diagnosed with Multiple Sclerosis (MS) but I cannot tell you when I received that diagnosis. But I can tell you it has totally taken over my life. It would be devastating news for anyone, but it was especially hard for me as I had become estranged from my family and my support was very limited and not healthy.

MS is a neurological disease that affects the nerves in the brain and spinal cord. I have gradually lost my ability to speak and my mobility. I do not know if anyone in my birth family had MS because I was adopted when I was a baby from an orphanage. I was not told of my adoption until I was older and learned from a friend of our family. My ability to speak gradually progressed to the point that my speech difficulties were now compounded by physical disabilities such as muscle weakness, tremors, and balance issues. I relied on a wheelchair to get around, and now I am not able to get out of bed by myself. Dr. Maya Angelou said it best *"still I rise."* I need assistance with daily tasks such as grooming and eating. I had been self-sufficient and to have to wait for someone to assist me can be very hard and depressing.

Despite these challenges, I refused to give up. I adapted to my new reality and found creative solutions to communicate and live my life to the fullest. I AM learning how to use that which will give me the freedom that has escaped me for over 15 years. I use an alphabet chart to spell out words and a picture board that allows me to point to different phrases and words when I need to express something quickly. I play computer games with my sister and take great pleasure in winning. I recently connected with childhood friends and even though I cannot speak, I do have a voice. It is a different kind of voice, one that requires more patience and understanding for myself and from those around me. But it is a voice nonetheless, and I am determined to use it to make a difference in the world. I am grateful for learning the importance of resilience and perseverance. I am also thankful for the advancements in technology and medicine that allow me to live a fulfilling life despite my abilities.

As I continue my journey through life with MS, I have faced many adversities and moments of despair. Including being placed in hospice. However, I have also experienced moments of triumph and joy. A couple of months back I had progressed to the point that I no longer need hospice care and to that I say thank you God. Through it all, I have learned valuable lessons that I would like to share with anyone facing their own challenges.

1. *Embrace your unique voice*: Each one of us has a unique voice and perspective to offer the world. It might not always be spoken words; it could be expressed through art, writing, or any other creative mediums.

2. *Embrace your individuality* and find ways to share your thoughts and feelings with the world.

3. *Seek support and understanding*: Surround yourself with people who are patient, understanding, and supportive. Seek out friends, family, or support groups that can offer a safe space for you to express yourself and share your experiences. Having a strong support network can make a world of difference during tough times.

4. *Adapt and innovate*: Life may throw unexpected challenges at us, but it is essential to adapt and find innovative solutions. Technology can be a powerful ally in overcoming obstacles, just like the picture board I use to communicate. Explore assistive technologies and devices that can help improve your quality of life.

5. *Practice resilience and perseverance*: Resilience is the ability to bounce back from difficult situations, and perseverance is the determination to keep moving forward despite setbacks. Cultivate these qualities in

yourself and remember that setbacks are a natural part of life's journey.

6. *Focus on what you can control:* While some things may be beyond our control, we can always choose how we respond to them. Having an attitude of gratitude elevates you. Concentrate on the aspects of life you can influence and let go of the things you cannot change. Not an easy task but also not impossible.

7. *Celebrate small victories:* In the face of adversity, celebrating even the tiniest accomplishments can be empowering. Each step forward, no matter how small, is progress worth acknowledging.

8. *Seek professional support:* Don't hesitate to seek help from healthcare professionals, therapists, or counselors if you need support in dealing with your situation. Professional guidance can provide valuable insights and coping strategies.

9. *Find purpose and meaning:* Discover what gives your life purpose and meaning. Engage in activities that bring you joy and fulfillment, even if they may need to be adapted to your circumstances.

10. *Educate and raise awareness:* Use your voice and experiences to raise awareness about your condition or any other issue you care about. By educating others, you can help foster understanding and empathy.

In conclusion, my journey reminds me that life's challenges do not define us; it is how we face them that truly matters. As you move forward through adversities, remember that you are not alone, and there are resources, support, and hope available to you. Embrace your unique voice, keep pushing forward, and never ever give up on your dreams. The human spirit is resilient, and with determination and support, you can overcome even the most significant obstacles.

My memory is not the best but here are a few of the scripture verses that have supported me through this journey.

1. Psalm 46:1 (NIV) – *"God is our refuge and strength, an ever-present help in trouble."*

2. 2 Corinthians 4:8-9 (NIV) – *"We are hard-pressed on every side, but not crushed; perplexed, but not in despair; persecuted, but not abandoned; struck down, but not destroyed."*

3. 1 Peter 5:7 (NIV) – *"Cast all your anxiety on him because he cares for you."*

These verses remind me that God is our source of strength, comfort, and hope in times of adversity. Turning to Him and trusting in His promises can bring solace and courage to face life's challenges. Remember that you are not alone, and God's love and grace are always available to help you through difficult times. I thank you for taking the time to read about my voice. I ask that you pray for me and those who have accepted the calling to support others who cannot care for themselves. I AM grateful to be able to contribute and pray you will continue to move forward; in spite of the challenges, you face.

With all of my heart I would like to thank what my sister has named *"Felicia's Angels"* – the staff of Harmony House Hospice – without their care I am sure I would not be alive to write this. Nurse Shannon C. of Haven Health in Tucson Arizona and the staff of Haven Health of Scottsdale Az.

To my family and friends – Deidre, Dean, Cam, Greg and Vicki! You are my rock and my cheerleaders, and I love you.

ABOUT AUTHOR
Felicia Calcoate

Felicia Calcoate, a late-discovery adoptee hailing from Chicago, Illinois, has dedicated the past decade to mastering the art of navigating life with Multiple Sclerosis (MS). Despite the challenges posed by MS, which have taken away her mobility and voice, Felicia is resiliently forging a fresh means of communication.

Connect with Felicia (Through her sister Dr. Deidre)

Www.gowithinnotwithout.com

Facebook – Deidre.a.calcoate

Instagram – dcalcoate

RISING UP FROM THE ASHES INTO WHO I WAS CREATED TO BE
By Megan Fortner

L et's start with what the ashes represent. The ashes are where I'm going through life, living with no real purpose and just getting by, battling depression, anxiety, anger, eating disorders, suicidal thoughts, no financial stability, trying to find love in all the wrong places, and being run over by people. Sound familiar to anyone?

My breaking and turning point to finally getting up out of the ashes came one day, sitting on a swing. I was sitting there feeling betrayed, hurt, unloved, unimportant, depressed, sad, financially depleted, and ready to be done with life. As I sat there in the ashes, trying to determine whether I wanted to continue to live or be done with life, the love of God surrounded me. No, I didn't know much about God at the time. I knew He existed, and I'd always heard I could have a better life if I chose him. However, it seemed like every time I chose Him, things would fall apart or get worse. I didn't realize that I had an adversary, the devil, who was trying to call me back to him when I tried to follow God.

As I sat on that swing, contemplating... am I going to stay in these ashes, am I gonna leave this world, or am I going to change my life? I could feel the love of God surrounding me. Suddenly, I didn't feel depressed or sad anymore. Then I heard on the inside, *"You may be done, but I'm not, and if you choose Me, I will give you the life I've intended for you all along."*

That was it for me. I was ready. I was empowered. I was loved so much that I was prepared to go out and change everything about myself and about my life. At this point, there is nothing that can stop me from finding out who God is, who I am, and what I have in Christ. Finding out what the life was that He had for me.

As I got up out of the ashes. I stood tall, my head up and my shoulders back, and said, *"God, I choose You! Show me how to get this better life. Show me who You created me to be, and I'm ready for whatever You have. I shook those ashes off and NEVER LOOKED BACK!"*

Because of my hunger and desire for this life, He told me about it; He said, *"I can sustain that hunger. I can quench that thirst to where you'll never be thirsty again. I will refine you and shape you while making you an advertisement for My glory!"* Are you catching where this is going? My next best me is going to emerge from these ashes, and it's only up from here—glory to God.

I said, *"OK, Lord, let's go."* Every day, I went to Him and said, "God, show me what I need to do! Show me what I need to let go of! Show me who I need in my life and who I need to let go of!" And you know what? He did just that. He showed me who He didn't want me to be anymore, that when I gave my life to Him, the old me that was depressed, sad, suicidal, battled eating disorders, feared, living day to day financially, and always tried to make everyone else happy was dead and gone. He showed me that He saved me from the ashes and is creating me into who I was always intended to be all along.

I'm not telling you that this is going to be easy! Your flesh and the devil will always try to pull you back into the world, old habits, or remind you of your past mistakes and failures. The devil is good at doing that when you are a newborn baby in Christ, waiver, or are not strong in faith. But, when you gave your life to God, you now have the Holy Spirit on the inside. You have the power to tell your feelings and thoughts no. You have the power to bind the attacks of the enemy by the Blood and name of Jesus.

Let me teach you how to walk into and become Your Next Best You. Are you ready? I know you are! I know you're tired of being stuck and held back. Well, let's dive in, rise up from the ashes of who you think you are, and tap into the unique, strong, loving, powerful warrior that God has intended for you to be ALL ALONG!

As you start this journey into your next best you, look at John 3:16. It says, *"For God so loved the world that He gave His only begotten Son, that whosoever believes in Him should NOT perish, but have everlasting life."* This shows you the sacrifice Jesus made for you and why He went to the cross. He went to the cross to die our death because of sin, and so we could be restored to fellowship, perfect soundness, and right standing before God. When we choose Him, we have everlasting life, direction, correction, and protection and will not perish. Wow, right? How amazing is knowing that you have a Father who loves you so much and would send His son to die for your sin so you don't have to do it? When you choose Him, you are restored to perfect fellowship with your creator. All your sins, past mistakes, and failures are forgiven. Your slate is fresh and new, with nothing wrong on it. He sees you as the child He has created you to be and is ready to raise you up in this world for His kingdom! Oh, that makes me soooo excited!

Let's look at 2 Corinthians 5:17. It says, *"Therefore, if any man is in Christ, he is a new creature. Old things have passed away. Look, everything has become new."* This scripture is telling you that you have become a whole new person. Who you once were is dead and gone. You are NOW a unique, new creation in Christ. There is no other person like you. You are one with Christ; now, His plan for your life is yours alone. No one can take that from you but you. The Bible says in Hebrews 12:1 that we are running a race that is marked out for us. You have your own race. You have your own purpose, and you have your OWN Next Best You. No one can take your race because it is tailor-made just for you. No one can take your place and purpose on this earth because it is yours for the taking. Hallelujah, right? To KNOW Your Next Best You starts with YOU and God. It's seeing what He has for you and taking every step He asks of you to get there. Wow!

I know, I know, the next question is… How do I find out what my purpose is? That's easy! Get in the Word, build a relationship with God, talk to Him, pray to Him, ask, and then be silent. The Bible says in Matthew 7:7,8, *"Ask and it will be given to you; seek and you shall find; knock and the door will be opened to you. For everyone who asks receives; the one who seeks finds; and to the one who knocks, the door will be opened."* When you ask, expect to receive your answer by Faith!

Get in the Word every day. Our faith and expectancy grow by hearing and hearing by the Word of God. You will start to see things in a whole different light. You will see that prosperity, peace, love, kindness, gentleness, generosity, self-control, and your purpose are already yours. You just have to tap into it. As you start to tap into your Next Best You, you will begin seeing your Next Best You come to life.

Now that you have asked got silent, and received, start to look up to people who have the life that you know you are called to have. Stop surrounding yourself with people or the environment you KNOW you're not supposed to be in or around. The Bible says, *"Bad company corrupts good character."* It's true. If you're wanting to tap into Your Next Best You, look around you. What do you see? Do you see failure, addiction, negativity, discouragement? The environment you surround yourself with, you start to be like!" I read a quote once that said, *"Find the people that's where you want to be and honor them; watch them!"* When you surround yourself with people who want the best for you, want you to succeed, and show you how to grow and succeed…. What are you going to do? BE SUCCESSFUL!

Now, what are YOU saying about yourself and your life? The Bible says in Mark 11:22,23, *"Have faith in God! Truly, I say to you, whoever says to this mountain, be thy removed and cast into the sea, and does not doubt in his heart, but believes what he says will come to pass, he will have what he says,"* You want to be prosperous? Say it and believe it in your heart! Prosperity is already yours as a child of God. If God tells you that it's yours, it's yours. Start saying it, believing it, and standing in it. The word says you will have what you say! What you say about your life, yourself, and your circumstances are important. You want to be your Next Best You? Say what God says about you, and that's it!

Let me give you some confessions in the Word that's yours: *"You're triumphant, you have the victory. You're seated in heavenly places far above all powers and principalities; you have the same power and authority as Christ because the Holy Spirit lives in you. You are blessed going in and blessed coming out. God never leaves you nor forsakes you. He gives the desires of your heart as long as you live according to His purpose. He supplies your every need according to His riches and glory. Everything your hands touch will prosper. He has land for you. No weapon formed again you shall prosper. The devil, his powers and principalities are under your feet. No one can curse what the Lord has blessed. You don't have a spirit of fear but of power, love, and a sound mind. You have the mind of Christ. The devil has no control over your life. He can no longer make you live in fear or have depression. He can no longer make you feel anxious. You're unstoppable with God on your side."*

When you follow God and step into your Next Best You, the devil will come and try to steal it or get you off course. He will send people and trials. Don't give into it or give up. The Bible says in John 16:3, *"In the world, you will have trials and tribulations, but be of good cheer, I (Jesus) overcame the world!"* That means so have you. You can laugh in the face of adversity, knowing the trying of your Faith works patience and endurance, letting patience have its perfect work in you as your endurance grows stronger. Then you will be perfect and entirely wanting NOTHING! (James 1:3,4) The devil CAN'T STOP you from becoming Your Next Best You unless you let him.

Your Next Best You is walking in the plan and purpose that God has for you. If you're Confused, depressed, anxious, fearful, sick, downcast, burdened, or shameful. You don't have to stay there. There is a higher purpose for you, and there is a better life. All it takes is saying yes, Lord. Have your way in me. I'm ready to step into MY NEXT BEST ME!

I am a living, breathing testimony to all of this. I became My Next Best Me by following these steps, knowing that the devil will do everything he can to stop it. When you know all things negative, shame, guilt, and sin come from him... You know how to combat it! Ephesians 6 talks about God's armor and putting it on every morning. Make sure to put it on by getting in the Word, God's presence, rejoicing, being full of joy, and powering up for the day! Let the Word be what comes out of your mouth in every situation. I once was deep in the ashes. Living life with the worldly desires.

Now, I have my own podcast and YouTube called Faith and Fire with Megan Fortner. I minister on Facebook, through Zooms, and on the radio. I'm a traveling minister who goes all over the United States preaching the Good News Gospel. I tell my testimony and help others worldwide know how to live by Faith, walk in love, who they are, what they have, and what they can do because they are in Christ. We have authority, and we WIN in this life.

NOW is your time. We only have today because tomorrow is never promised. So, I ask you……. Are you ready to become your NEXT BEST YOU?

ABOUT AUTHOR
Megan Fortner

Megan Fortner is a woman, on fire, after God's heart and plan for her life. Megan is very passionate about showing God's love and teaching others who they are and what they have in Christ.

Megan graduated ICIBC through Mark Hankins Ministers in February 2021. Since then, she has been traveling, bringing the Word over the radio and on social media! Anywhere God wants her to go or be, she is. Megan is currently working for Mark Hankins Ministries and loves it. There is no other place she wants to be!

Megan and her husband, Dustin, own their own outfitting business, Driven Purpose Outfitting, because it's all about the outdoors, hunting and God! They LOVE to hunt, and so do their boys. It's in their blood!

Megan is a coach at heart for the Kingdom of God and for basketball. She has been coaching 3rd-6th grade for six years. Teaching and leading are her passion. It's in her heart!

Currently in the works is a podcast, YouTube channel, and an app for her ministry. God's ways are higher than ours, and Megan is just honored to be the vessel!

Megan is a wife of an amazing husband and a momma to two amazing little boys, Ruger (8) and Kiaus (5). They all are currently living in Northern Missouri.

Connect with Megan

Drivenwithapurpose@yahoo.com

Facebook: Megan Fortner

FROM BROKENNESS TO A GOLDEN REPAIR
By Claudine Hicks

In the depths of my brokenness, I found myself trapped in a constant search for love in all the wrong places. Relationship after relationship left me feeling broken, hurt, empty, and unworthy. I believed that if I could find the right person, the pain of my past would fade away, and I would finally feel complete. However, with each disappointment, the void within me grew deeper and deeper, and I realized that the love and fulfillment I sought from others could never truly heal my brokenness. It was only when I experienced the unconditional love of Jesus Christ and how He sees me that I discovered the path to a golden repair. My brokenness was an open door to experience Yeshua's unconditional love.

Webster's Dictionary defines brokenness as a state of being uneven or shattered, often manifesting as a broken heart which describes my early life, which was flawed by deep wounds, hurt, emptiness, and broken.

My journey began with a continual search for love in all the wrong places. I believed that finding the perfect relationship would fill the emptiness within me and validate my worth. However, each failed attempt left me feeling more broken, unworthy, and empty. It was a painful cycle that kept repeating until I reached a breaking point and realized that the love I sought externally could never truly mend my brokenness.

Brokenness can also be a beautiful entry point for healing to flow through. It is a place to find Freedom, where the hurting, broken places make way for open doors of love to flow. It is where oil can reach the deepest ache and be released as beauty from having been pressed down, tried, and crushed. Brokenness becomes a place where the glory of God can restore the shattered pieces to something even better than before. It is a place where we allow ourselves to receive, be ministered to, and be restored.

At 16, I had my first child, Caressa, who was born prematurely and had to stay in the hospital until she was at the proper weight to come home. While carrying her, I still attended school, determined to create a future despite the challenges and choices I made in life. After Caressa was released from the hospital, I continued my education, this time attending night school so I could graduate with my High School class.

Let me add that after I had Caressa, I vowed to the Lord that the next person I laid with would be my husband. When

I said those words and made that commitment, I believed it wholeheartedly. However, life had other plans. I reconnected with an ex, and not long after, I found out that I was pregnant again. Panic set in; I was afraid to tell my mom and my brother. I shared this news with the young man the day I left the clinic, and he promised to discuss it, but sadly, he disappeared after I shared the news.

Once again, I had mistaken attention for love, and I found myself in a daunting situation, raising an infant and crying myself to sleep almost every night, trying to figure out what to do. I even considered the unthinkable, despite being against abortion, for I was a scared young girl who felt alone. How could I bring another child into this world when I didn't even know my own identity or what my future would look like? Surely this baby deserved better.

I remember crying out to God, pleading for help, desperately seeking a way out of the darkness that seemed to suffocate me; about two weeks after finding out that I was pregnant, while in my Science class, a sharp pain tore through my abdomen. I tried to ignore it, but the pain intensified, and I felt what seemed like the start of my period. I rushed to the restroom, blood staining my clothes along the way.

Upon returning to the class, my teacher noticed something was wrong, and I was allowed to leave early. That's when I called a close friend who urged me to go to the hospital to prevent going into shock. *"You are having a miscarriage,"* she said. I was scared, lost, and waiting anxiously by the steps for her to pick me up. By the time I reached the hospital, the pain had escalated to an excruciating level. I shared my suspicions of having a miscarriage, and they quickly took me to a room.

I don't remember much from that moment, but I do remember waking up and seeing my mom's face in the back of the room praying. She had been notified because I was under 18. There I lay, in a hospital bed, undergoing a D&C procedure, a process to clear the uterine lining after a miscarriage.

Never did I think I would find myself in this position so soon. My baby was still in diapers. It was a heart-wrenching experience, and for years, I carried the weight of that trauma. I silently wrestled with my emotions, not speaking of it much back then, but always thinking about Rachel, the name my Heavenly Father gave my precious princess in Heaven. I know now that she is a beautiful girl and in Heaven's nursery, and I will get to hold her one day.

Time moved forward, and life presented its opportunities, yet I continued to make puzzling choices in my relationships with men. I became actively involved in the church I had grown up in, joining various ministries and hoping to find identity and purpose. However, where Yeshua, my Savior, met me was not within the walls of the church or at a church meeting.

The turning point came when I encountered the unconditional love of Jesus Christ. In the midst of my brokenness and despair, I experienced a love that surpassed all understanding. Yeshua embraced my flaws, accepted me as I was, and revealed my inherent worthiness. In this encounter, I learned that there is nothing and no one too far gone for God to restore.

I recall a specific day that wasn't marked by a church service or an altar call. It was a day when I found myself in my room, overwhelmed and at the end of my rope. I was a wreck, crying with those hot tears streaming down my cheeks. I reached out to one of the mothers of the Church, and though she was busy, she said she would return my call later. After waiting for a few hours, she never returned my call. I did the only thing I knew to do next: I called on Jesus.

I was transparent with Jesus, laying bare all the broken pieces of my soul at HIS feet. I was done with life's empty pursuits. I was done with relationships as I had known them, but deep down, I knew that only Yeshua could bring healing to those shattered parts. And at that moment, HE met me there.

"From Brokenness to a Golden Repair" is more than a chapter; it's a vibrant tapestry woven from the threads of my own life. It's a tale of grappling with brokenness, the pursuit of love in all the wrong corners, and the stunning revelation of God's unconditional love, a force so powerful it has transformed me into My Next Best Me.

Imagine, just like the ancient art of Kintsugi, where broken pottery is repaired with gold, silver, or platinum, highlighting the very cracks that once marred its surface. In the same way, this journey, this metamorphosis from brokenness to becoming our most exquisite selves, is like our very beings are being adorned with the gold of restoration. Yes, Restoration!

As we venture forth on this journey of transformation, my prayer is that you'll not only find hope but a wellspring of inspiration. I hope you'll discover a renewed sense of purpose, an awakening within your spirit, and a profound understanding that brokenness is not an end but a remarkable beginning. It's a gateway, a portal through which the beauty that resides deep within you can be lovingly restored and then unleashed upon the world, radiant and unstoppable.

As my journey unfolded, a profound principle emerged from the depths of my experiences—an awakening that shattered the illusion I had been chasing. The continuous quest for love and validation from external sources, oh, it was a mirage, a fleeting shadow that left me with nothing but pain and disappointment. The path to true healing and lasting wholeness, I've established, is not to be found in the arms of another human, but in the embrace of a higher power, in the radiant light of a love so unconditional, it's almost beyond comprehension.

This love, this glorious, unbounded love, it finds its embodiment in the person of Jesus Christ. This love is where I found that I am the beloved of Elohim, the ONE who gazes upon me with eyes that know my very soul, who accepts me despite my flaws, but wholly, without a hint of judgment. It's through this exquisite relationship with Him, the one who knows me better than I know ourselves, that I unearth my true worth, and that is the key to the golden repair.

Kintsugi involves repairing broken pottery with a special lacquer mixed with gold, silver, or platinum, transforming the objects into something more beautiful than they were before. It serves as a metaphor for healing and personal growth, highlighting that even in our brokenness, we have the potential to become something greater.

Reflect on your own quest for love and validation. Acknowledge the pain and disappointment that came from seeking it in the wrong places. Embrace the realization that the repair you seek lies not in others but in your relationship with Jesus. Shift your focus from external sources of love to cultivating a deep and intimate connection with Jesus Christ.

Embrace the unconditional love and acceptance that Jesus Christ offers. Cultivate a deep and intimate relationship with Him through prayer, worship, meditation, and His word. Seek guidance and support from individuals who have experienced the transformative power of His love. Allow this love to permeate every aspect of your being, healing your brokenness and restoring your sense of worth.

The word "*repair*" carries the essence of restoration, rebuilding, and irreversible mending. It is a concept that resonates deeply with the journey from brokenness to a golden repair. Just as broken pottery can be repaired using a special lacquer mixed with gold, silver, or platinum in the Japanese art form known as kintsugi, we, too, have the potential to be mended and transformed into something more beautiful than before.

The philosophy behind kintsugi teaches us that brokenness does not have to be a state of permanent despair. Instead, it is an opportunity for growth and personal evolution. The cracks and imperfections become part of our unique story, making us even more resilient and beautiful.

In the same way, the journey from brokenness to becoming a kintsugi masterpiece is a metaphor for the process of healing and personal growth. It involves recognizing that even though we may be broken, we have the potential to become something even better. The golden repair symbolizes the transformation that occurs when we embrace our brokenness, mend our wounds, and allow the love of Jesus to fill and strengthen us.

This has been a remarkable transformative journey from the depths of brokenness to the radiant glory of a golden repair, and there's a truth I want you to carry in your heart: this venture is your very own, uniquely personal pursuit. As you read and absorb the principles woven through the tapestry of this book, let them take root in your soul; let them guide your steps toward a profound transformation. But remember, transformation is a journey, one that requires a Yes to Jesus as you invite Him into those hidden places. HE is waiting for you, and HE is in no way afraid of your mess.

In the midst of these pages, you've discovered the radiant love of Jesus Christ, a love that holds the power to mend, restore, and illuminate. The repair you seek is not far off in the distance; it resides within the very fabric of your being, waiting to be uncovered and fully embraced.

Picture this, just like the ancient art of kintsugi, where the broken fragments of pottery are lovingly mended with delicate threads of gold, silver, or platinum. These repairs don't hide the scars; they elevate them into symbols of resilience and stunning beauty. It's a metaphor that mirrors our own journey—our brokenness, when touched only by the hands of our Heavenly Father, becomes not just mended, but transformed, a beautiful story etched with the grace of your Heavenly Father.

As you stand at the threshold of this journey, know that you don't have to do this walk alone. I encourage you to partner with the Father, the Son, and the Holy Spirit. Together, you embark on a journey to not only discover your own golden repair but to be a beacon for others. You are called to share the truth that brokenness is not the end; it's the beginning of a magnificent story where you can receive beauty from the ashes.

And let's remember that the golden repair we long for is not a distant dream; it's within our grasp, within the very reach of our spirits. In becoming Your Next Best You, you aren't just transforming yourself; you're unleashing a ripple effect of transformation in the lives you touch, and that is a beautiful legacy.

As I reflect on my own journey, I'm deeply grateful for the privilege of being My Next Best Me, a partnership forged with the Father, the Son, and the Holy Spirit. In this divine alliance, I've not only found my true identity as a Daughter of my Heavenly Father but have also realized that I am royalty and that my life is a daily journey of growth and discovery. This journey is not just about being saved and free; it's about the exquisite realization that we are heirs to an everlasting kingdom. We are Royalty. With this understanding, let's embrace our sacred purpose; let's walk this path with a sense of regal courage and grace, knowing that we are destined for a life adorned with the beauty of transformation.

God made my life complete when I placed all the pieces
before him.
When I got my act together, he gave me a fresh start.
Now I'm alert to God's ways, I don't take God for granted.
Every day I review the ways he works; I try not to miss a trick.
I feel put back together, and I'm watching my step.
God rewrote the text of my life when I opened the book of my heart
to his eyes.

Psalm 18:20-24

"I knew you before I placed YOU in your mother's womb."

Jeremiah 1:5

ABOUT AUTHOR
Claudine Hicks

With a decade of experience as a Freedom & Meditation Coach, Author, and Speaker, Claudine Hicks, founder of Au·then·ti·ꓘal·ly You Coaching, is driven by a deep passion for helping others uncover their authentic identity as they navigate the path to Freedom.

Through years of working with and mentoring young women from around the world, she has developed a unique coaching approach that enables clients to recognize their true identity as daughters and walk in Freedom.

Her ultimate goal is to help her clients embrace their authentic selves and celebrate their unique qualities. Inspired by the Japanese art of Kintsugi, she believes that everyone is a golden repair, and that even brokenness can become part of a beautiful story. Her vision for her clients is to help them realize they can live truly authentic lives and be who God originally created them to be.

As a coach, Claudine uses Biblical principles as the foundation for her coaching sessions. She invites the guidance of the Holy Spirit to help her clients rewrite their stories with a God-inspired ending.

As an author, she has published several books on topics related to personal growth and self-discovery. Her work has been recognized by publications such as Emerging Leaders Magazine, Voyage ATL Magazine, and Shout Out Atlanta. Claudine has also been a guest on several TV shows and podcasts, discussing her expertise and wisdom with a diverse audience.

Claudine's expertise has been acknowledged through her participation as a featured presenter at the prestigious 10th Annual Sister to Sister G.L.O.W Conference in Rockford, IL. Her impactful presentations have left a lasting impact on the attendees.

Moreover, Claudine delivered a compelling speech at a remarkable event held in Jamaica. Addressing over 400 high school students, Claudine's inspiring words ignited a passion for personal growth and skill-building during their annual Skill Building event. Her impactful message resonated deeply with the young minds, empowering them to embrace their potential and pursue their dreams.

At the core of Claudine's mission is her motto, "Made Free To Set Free," which encapsulates her dedication to helping individuals break free from the chains of past hurts, trauma, and negative beliefs. This enables them to live authentically and fulfill their divine purpose as daughters of God.

To connect with Claudine or explore her transformative work at Au·then·ti·)al·ly You Coaching, you can reach out via:

Email: Claudine@claudinehicks.com

Linktree: https://linktr.ee/claudinehicks

THE POWER OF FAITH
By Dr. Wilnord Louis Charles

"Truly, I tell you, if you have faith as small as a mustard seed, you can say to this mountain, 'Move from here to there,' and it will move. Nothing will be impossible for you."
Matthew 17:20

Faith is a powerful and motivating force that can help people move from *nothing to something*. It is one of the most powerful forces in the universe; it is the essence of life. Nothing is possible without faith. Faith can provide the necessary tools to overcome obstacles and achieve success. Personal experiences can sometimes be the driving force behind an individual's faith, which is the case with me. I was born and raised in Haiti in a poor family. Our living conditions were far from ideal- we were eight persons living in a one small bedroom home with a dirt floor, and at this time, the ten closest houses in our neighborhood were dirt floors, including my two grandmother's houses.

My dad was only 19 when he got married, and he had me at 20. He grew up with a single mother; the last time he saw his dad was six years old. He understood firsthand the difficulties of poverty. My mother also grew up in miserable conditions without her father's support. My heart always aches as I recount the painful journey my mother faced while growing up without a father. Her mother, unable to take care of her and her six other siblings, had no choice but to separate my mother and her siblings among different households. Thus began her tumultuous childhood, marked by hardship and mistreatment.

Despite being the youngest, ten years old, in some houses she lived in, my mother was forced to bear the responsibility of caring for other kids way older than her. Each day was a struggle as she faced physical and emotional abuse. One fateful day, she unintentionally added too much salt to a meal, a mistake that invoked the wrath of the man she resided with. His rage knew no bounds as he mercilessly attacked her, landing five brutal punches on her nose. Blood flowed like a wounded animal, and to add insult to her injury, the man pissed on her assaulted head, causing her to lose consciousness for hours.

As I reflect on this heartbreaking story, tears well up in my eyes. It is a reminder of the immense strength and resilience my mother possesses. Her unwavering love for her children motivated me to strive for greatness as I yearned to provide her with the life she deserved.

A Sacrificial and Miraculous Birth

In a small remote village, my mother braved the trials of her first childbirth, my birth. For nine agonizing days, she endured acute pain with no medical assistance in sight. Our family, afflicted by poverty, couldn't afford the luxury of a hospital. My mother and I were really close to death. With each passing day, hope was replaced by despair. But in the middle of the darkness, my dad's unwavering faith persisted. God answered our prayers on the ninth day like a heavenly intervention. A miracle unfolded as the sun dipped below the horizon, casting a golden glow across the horizon. Guided by an inherent strength, my mother assembled every ounce of bravery she possessed. With sheer determination, she pushed, drawing upon an immense reservoir of love and devotion. In that dimly lit room, sweat poured down her furrowed brow as she fought valiantly. And then, amid a symphony of pain, a cry echoed through the air, announcing my arrival.

Tears of relief streaked down my mother's face, mixing with her perspiration. Her joy knew no bounds as she clutched me to her chest, feeling a newfound purpose coursing through her veins. Once filled with apprehension, the room was transformed into a sanctuary of triumph. Her story became a reminder that even in the darkest times, the human spirit can overcome the greatest odds.

As I grew older, my mother's story was a constant source of inspiration for me. Every milestone, every achievement, I owe them to my mother.

Prayer Works Miracles

My dad's greatest tool was always prayer. Despite the overwhelming obstacles we were facing, my dad's faith never wavered, and he instilled in us the belief that through prayer and education, we could rise above our circumstances. His unwavering determination and faith have been the foundation of our family's resilience and growth. My parents have always believed that tomorrow will be better. I am so fortunate that this book will come out at a time when they are alive. I write this book to honor them, for they have taught me one of the greatest values in life, *"Faith."*

The Land of The Familiar

Faith requires that we take the courage to move out from the land of the familiar, which is our current situation or our past. The Bible in Romans 12 verse 2 addresses this recommendation, *"Do not conform to the pattern of the world but be transformed by the renewing of our mind."* Changing our thinking about who we are is an essential part of our Next Best Life. The same kind of thinking will produce the same type of results unless we change them.

As humans, we have the tendency to ignore God's plan for our lives and focus on our actual situation or to dwell on our past situations. We often forget that the bible says that our current situation is temporary; nothing lasts forever. But Sometimes we are too busy living in the past, and we often neglect God's plan for our life that He clearly mentions in Jeremiah 29 verse 11, *"'For I know the plans I have for you,' declares the Lord, 'plans to prosper you and not to harm you, plans to give you a hope and a future.'"*

At the lowest point in my life, I always remind myself about God's plan for my life. In fact, my life has been a series of stories that revolve around faith, and it has been a source of strength and motivation, leading me to achieve my goals.

Tested Faith

Faith is often seen as a powerful force that compels us to persevere through challenging times. The statement, *"faith not tested cannot be trusted,"* holds true in my personal experience, particularly during my college years. It was a time when my financial situation was incredibly difficult, and my faith was put to the ultimate test.

During this period, my family faced a severe financial crisis, and my parents were no longer able to support my education expenses. The burden fell on my shoulders, and I was left to figure out a way to make ends meet. Unfortunately, the situation became so dire that I found myself unable to pay my rent. With no other option, I approached a close friend of mine, who graciously allowed me to sleep on the floor in his tiny room, right in front of his bed. As if that was not enough, my belongings had to be stored at another friend's house due to the lack of space.

In the face of these seemingly insurmountable challenges, my faith became my anchor. It was the unwavering belief that I could overcome this situation and succeed that kept me going. Instead of giving up on my dreams, I persevered and focused on my studies. I spent countless nights burning the midnight oil, determined not to let my circumstances define my future.

Eventually, my faith and hard work paid off. I managed to complete all my classes with excellent grades and secure a job at the bank, the first one in my family having a salary, that not only allowed me to sustain myself but also support my family. With my newfound financial opportunity, I was able to alleviate my parents' debts and contribute to the well-being of my younger siblings.

This experience made me realize the true power of faith. In times of adversity, having faith in oneself and a higher power provides the strength and motivation needed to push through even the most challenging situations. It taught me that when our faith is tested and we persevere, our belief and our abilities become unwavering.

The Confidence to Move To our Next Best

There comes a time in our lives when we realize that we are meant for something great, something more. We feel a calling to take a step forward, to make a move, and to pursue the life that we have always dreamt of. But often, we get held back by our fears, doubts, and insecurities. The first step toward faith is to have self-confidence, which is believing in yourself. Doctor Norman Vincent Pearl, in his book *"The Power of Positive Thinking,"* in the first chapter, *"Believe In Yourself,"* has a great formula that can help us gain the confidence to get to our next best. He suggested one of the most powerful formulas, which is a sure cure for lack of confidence, is the thought that God is actually with you and helping you. This is one of the simplest teachings in religion, namely, that Almighty God will be your companion, will stand by you, help you, and see you through. To practice it, simply affirm, *"God is with me; God is helping me; God is guiding me."*

Faith Versus Fear

"You either pray or worry, but do not do both," says the American singer 50 Cents.

Fear and faith are two opposite forces; they cannot cohabitate. We all have fear. Fear by itself is not the problem, the issue is how we respond to it. Fear is a natural response to the unknown and often a product of past negative experiences. On the other hand, faith is a conviction in the goodness of the future and a belief that things will work out for the best. To move from fear to faith, one must first acknowledge one's fears and work on letting them go.

Moving from fear to faith is a journey of transformation that requires a shift in perspective. The good news is it is something that we can build. Our faith is the most important part of our life; fear could become the same if allowed. As humans, we have the power to build up this spiritual muscle called faith, or we can amplify our lives with this psychologically destructive liar called fear. Facing our fear can help us discover who we really are. I like this quote by Susan Jeffers, *"Feel the fear and do it anyway."* When we finally hit our terror barrier, we realized that our Next Best Life was always on the other side of our fear, and there was nothing to be afraid of.

Step Up For Your Destiny

Most of the time, we tend to underestimate who we are and who God has created us to be. You are God's child, the children of the almighty God. We were born champions, and we already possess everything that we need to win the game of life and become Our Next Best. What you allow your mind to see is what you will get. My dad always taught me about positive self-talk. This was one of the greatest assets I got from him. He said your word is the tool that can transform your life. You are more than what you see just take a step of faith toward your Next Best You.

Getting Started

One of the most valuable principles of faith my dad has taught me is the importance of getting started, even when things seem uncertain. There have been times in my life when I felt overwhelmed and unsure of what direction to take next, especially when it came to starting a new school year or planning for the future. However, my dad would always remind me that the hardest part is often just getting started. He would encourage me to take the first step, no matter how small, in the direction I wanted to go. This principle has helped me overcome my fears and take action, even when I didn't see the end in sight. With my dad's encouragement, I have learned to trust the process and believe that, as long as I take action and keep moving forward, I will eventually reach my goals.

The Comfort Zone

The comfort zone is where we feel safe and secure, doing things we are familiar with and avoiding anything that may be slightly challenging. However, staying in this zone for an extended period can be dangerous, as it can lead to stagnation and a sense of satisfaction.

Living life within the comfort zone prevents us from experiencing new opportunities and limits personal growth. It is easy to get trapped in a cycle of routine and become resistant to change. The longer we stay in our comfort zone, the more we lose the ability to adapt and take risks. This can result in missed opportunities and prevent us from reaching our full potential. Therefore, it is important to break out of our comfort zone, embrace the unknown, and try new things. Pushing past our fears and comfort can help us achieve our goals and lead more fulfilling lives.

In the final pages of my chapter book, I reflect upon the incredible journey of how the power of faith has transformed my life. As I recount the ups and downs, the challenges and triumphs, one thing becomes abundantly clear, faith has been my guiding light through it all.

Through faith, I have found solace in times of despair, strength in moments of weakness, and hope when all seemed lost. It is through my unwavering belief in God, the creator of the universe, that I have been able to persevere and rise above adversity.

But faith is not just about personal growth; it is about the profound impact it has on my relationships and interactions with others. Through faith, I have learned the transformative power of forgiveness, compassion, and love. It has taught me to see the beauty in every soul, to extend a helping hand to those in need, and to walk a path of kindness and understanding.

As I bring my chapter book to a close, I am overwhelmed with gratitude for the power of faith in my life. It has brought me clarity, direction, and a deep sense of purpose. It has ignited a fire within me, urging me to live a life of meaning and service to others.

With each turned page, I hope to inspire others to embrace faith in their own lives, for it is a force that can transcend boundaries, heal wounds, and illuminate the darkest of paths. Together, let us embark on a journey guided by faith, love, and the belief in the extraordinary power of God that lies within us all.

ABOUT AUTHOR
Dr. Wilnord Louis Charles

Wilnord Louis Charles is a Haitian-born author, speaker, and advocate for the power of faith and positive thinking. Raised in a family of six, Wilnord grew up in Haiti where he learned the importance of resilience, perseverance, and the power of faith.

At the age of 33, Wilnord moved to the United States, fulfilling one of his lifelong dreams. Starting from scratch in a new country was not easy, but he used his positive mindset and faith to guide him through the difficult times. This experience shaped his perspective on life, and he has since made it his mission to inspire others to adopt a similar mindset.

Wilnord's passion for personal development and motivation led him to be coached by some of the greatest motivational speakers on earth, Les Brown, Lisa Nichols, Jon Talarico and etc... The skills and knowledge he gained from those mentors fueled his desire to help others achieve success in their lives.

Wilnord is grateful for his supportive family, including his wife and children, who have been an inspiration on his journey. His commitment to helping others achieve success through faith, positive thinking, and personal development has made him an admired figure in the world of motivational speaking and writing.

Wilnord Louis Charles's chapter, "The Power of Faith," is a testament to his experiences and his message of hope for anyone seeking to achieve their dreams. Through his writing, Wilnord shares his wisdom and advice on how to adopt a positive mindset, stay motivated, and overcome obstacles in life. His words of encouragement and inspiration have touched the lives of many, and he continues to inspire and impact countless others with his message of hope and faith.

Connect with Wilnord

Social media:
IG: lwilnord
Facebook: wilnord Louis Charles
& wlc academy of greatness

EMBRACING JOY IN YOUR *NEXT*

By Nichol Perricci

D o you know what joy feels like? Is it a heart condition? An exhibition? Is it something you feel, something that's bleeding, or is it just something that comes and goes, dependent on the people around you? I honestly couldn't have told you about it a few years ago.

This book is coming out about a few years after our lovely pandemic. And it was in that pandemic that I discovered my next. Sounds crazy, right? Who grows a business out of a pandemic? Me, apparently. But in that pandemic, I would say, my family, in itself, got closer. Because you didn't have anything else to do, honestly."

Before the pandemic, I had defined myself by the roles I played in other people's lives. I was Jeff's mum, Bri's mom, Dre's mom, Donato's wife, the Youth Pastor's Wife. My identity was intricately woven with the lives of those around me. But when the pandemic hit, my children were either adults or almost there. Two of them were adults with lives of their own, one almost ready to graduate, and suddenly, I was faced with a daunting question: Who am I without these roles?

I realized I had to find myself in the midst of it all. What I discovered was that my happiness had always been dependent on external factors. It was a fragile, painted-on happiness that came and went with the presence of my loved ones. When they were around, I was content. When they were gone, I was lost.

This pattern wasn't new to me. As a divorced mom, I experienced the emptiness of an empty house when my kids were with their father. I had always sought distractions because I couldn't bear being alone with my own thoughts. It wasn't until the pandemic forced me to confront this reality that I realized I had been miserable for a long time.

The turning point came during one of the most challenging times in my life—a personal crisis involving one of my children. During this dark period, I had to detach myself from the situation, look within, and reevaluate my definition of happiness.

I discovered that there's a significant difference between being happy and having joy. Happiness is often fleeting, tied to circumstances and people. On the other hand, joy is a heart condition, a deep-seated feeling that remains constant regardless of external circumstances. It's a spiritual gift that comes from within, a connection between you and a higher power, unshaken by the storms of life. I had relied on the happiness painted on for all to see for so many years, and it was exhausting!

Choosing joy doesn't mean pretending everything is perfect or ignoring your struggles. It means acknowledging that God has you, even in the darkest moments. It means finding moments of joy in the midst of grief and pain and understanding that those who have left your life wouldn't want their absence to define your existence.

One of the times in my life that this was so very evident to me was quite a few years ago, during my daughter's junior year of high school, we received devastating news – her father, my ex-husband, had been involved in a horrific and ultimately fatal accident. This sudden tragedy was something I never anticipated having to navigate with her. At his funeral, as we spent a few moments with him before the service, her grandmother turned to her and said, *"Alright, no more tears; now it's time to celebrate your dad."* It was an incredibly challenging moment for me, as I couldn't simply switch off my emotions. However, it became evident that, for that day, they needed to wear a brave face to get through the service. This experience served as a profound lesson for both my daughter and me – the lesson of putting on a cheerful facade for the sake of others, especially when people are unsure of how to handle such situations. It was only after everyone had left that we allowed ourselves to grieve.

My daughter's loss taught me this lesson all too well. We still mourn her father's passing but also celebrate the joyous memories we shared with him. Choosing joy isn't about denying reality; it's about finding strength in your faith and knowing that you can weather any storm with grace.

When the pandemic started, and we found ourselves confined to our homes, I received a divine mission that year – consciously choose joy every morning, regardless of the circumstances. Initially, I thought it would be a breeze; after all, how hard could it be, right? But soon enough, I realized that some mornings proved challenging, and even if I had started the day with the intention of choosing joy, it often felt elusive by lunchtime. So, yes, I had to make a deliberate effort to choose joy consistently. This didn't mean that life's challenges vanished; instead, it meant that I committed to actively seeking joy amidst whatever was happening. It's not about denying life's realities; it's about recognizing that joy is always present, even in the midst of chaos. So, I made the choice to embrace joy wholeheartedly.

By embracing joy, I transformed my life. I started a business, found fulfillment in helping others, and cherished every moment with my family. I no longer depended on external circumstances or people for my happiness. Instead, I discovered an inner wellspring of joy that sustained me through life's challenges.

Choosing joy is a daily practice, a conscious decision to see the good in each day and respond to adversity with grace. It's about recognizing that happiness is fleeting, but joy is eternal. I challenge you to try it, to keep a journal, and find moments of joy in your daily life. It's a small change that can lead to profound transformation, a shift that will help you embrace joy and blessings in your journey forward.

As I delved deeper into this journey of embracing joy, I uncovered some key principles that have continued to shape my life. One of the most important realizations was how my choice to embrace joy impacted my mental and emotional well-being and physical health.

Living in a state of joy, I discovered, had tangible benefits for my health. The stress and negativity that had once consumed me began to dissipate. Studies have shown chronic stress can wreak havoc on the body, leading to various health problems. But by choosing joy, I reduced my stress levels and allowed my body to heal and thrive.

I also found that embracing joy had a profound impact on my relationships. When I was unhappy and reactive, my interactions with others often reflected that negativity. I had a short fuse and would react to situations rather than respond thoughtfully. This strained my relationships and left me feeling isolated.

However, as I practiced choosing joy, I became more patient, understanding, and compassionate in my interactions with others. I learned to respond to challenges with grace and empathy, fostering stronger and more meaningful connections with those around me. I began to radiate positivity, which, in turn, attracted positive people into my life.

Moreover, choosing joy allowed me to fully appreciate and cherish the moments I spent with my family and loved ones. It wasn't just about being happy when they were around but about finding joy in every interaction, regardless of the circumstances. I learned to live in the present, savoring each moment as a precious gift.

I often think back to the quote, "Today, I choose joy." My daughter-in-law made me a cup with this phrase, which serves as a daily reminder of my commitment to joy. Repetition is key to instilling change in our lives, and I chose to see this phrase every morning as I drink my iced tea. It became a symbol of my transformation and a beacon of positivity.

Choosing joy is a daily practice that, over time, becomes a way of life. It rewires your thought patterns and outlook on the world. It teaches you to see beauty in the ordinary, to find gratitude amid challenges, and to believe in the power of resilience.

In essence, embracing joy is a journey of self-discovery, a path to unlocking your true potential. It's a journey that has allowed me to grow, evolve, and become the best version of myself. So, I extend this challenge to you: Try choosing joy for a week, a month, or even longer. Document your journey, and I promise you'll see positive changes in your life that you never thought possible.

In the end, by embracing joy, you'll find happiness within yourself and radiate it out into the world, spreading positivity and light to those around you. Blessings on your journey toward embracing joy and discovering the boundless happiness that lies within you.

As my journey toward embracing joy continued, I realized that this transformation extended beyond the individual level. It had a ripple effect that touched the lives of those around me, ultimately leading to a more harmonious and joyful community.

One of the most significant changes I observed was how my newfound sense of joy influenced my relationships with my family. In the past, I had been so focused on the roles I played as a mother and wife that I often neglected my own well-being. I mistakenly believed that sacrificing my happiness for the sake of my family was the right thing to do.

However, through the process of choosing joy, I discovered that by prioritizing my own happiness and well-being, I could be a better mother, wife, and friend. I became more present, more patient, and more understanding. I no longer relied on my family to fulfill me; instead, I brought my own inner joy to our interactions.

This shift had a profound impact on my family dynamics. We laughed more, communicated better, and supported each other through life's ups and downs. I realized that when I embraced joy, I created a positive and loving atmosphere in my home.

But the impact of embracing joy didn't stop at my front door. I noticed that my newfound positivity and resilience also extended to my friendships and social interactions. I became a source of support and inspiration for my friends, who often turned to me for advice on how to find their own joy.

It was during this time that I realized the power of choosing joy as a force for good in the world. I started volunteering and helping those less fortunate, using my newfound perspective to bring hope and happiness to others. I realized that joy was not just a personal journey but also a way to impact the lives of those around me positively.

My business also flourished as I embraced joy. I found that my genuine passion for helping others achieve their goals resonated with my clients. I approached my work with enthusiasm and a desire to make a difference in their lives.

This authenticity and joy attracted clients to me, allowing my business to grow organically.

Choosing joy in my professional life also opened up new opportunities. I collaborated with like-minded individuals and organizations, expanding my reach and impact. I realized that success follows naturally when you approach your work with joy and a sense of purpose.

As my journey continued, I couldn't help but reflect on the broader implications of embracing joy. I saw how my choices rippled out into the world, touching the lives of others and inspiring them to choose joy as well. It became clear to me that joy was not just a personal pursuit but a collective one, a movement that could transform communities and societies.

I look forward to advocating for the importance of joy in various forums and publications, sharing my story, and encouraging others to embark on their journeys of embracing joy. I love working with people from different backgrounds and circumstances who reached out to me, sharing their stories of how choosing joy had transformed their lives. It was heartwarming to witness the impact of this simple yet profound choice on so many lives.

One of the key lessons I learned during this journey was that choosing joy wasn't about denying or ignoring life's challenges. It was about facing them with a positive mindset, resilience, and unwavering faith. I encountered my fair share of obstacles, setbacks, and moments of doubt, but I never wavered in my commitment to joy.

I also realized that joy wasn't a destination but a continuous journey. Life is filled with highs and lows, and embracing joy meant navigating both with grace and gratitude. It meant finding joy in the small moments—the sun's warmth on my face, a heartfelt conversation with a friend, or the laughter of my grandbabies.

Choosing joy had become a way of life, a guiding principle that shaped my thoughts, actions, and relationships. It allowed me to become the best version of myself, to inspire positive change in those around me, and to find purpose and fulfillment in my work.

As I look back on this transformative journey, I am filled with gratitude for the lessons I've learned and the joy I've discovered. I am reminded of the power of choice, the power to choose joy in the face of adversity and uncertainty. I have learned that true happiness is choosing joy. If you have real happiness, you have found the meaning of true joy.

I leave you with this challenge: Embrace joy in your NEXT, not as a fleeting emotion, but as a deep-seated state of being. Choose joy daily, even when life's challenges loom large. Share your joy with others, for it has the power to inspire and uplift. And remember that in the embrace of joy, you'll find not only happiness but also purpose, resilience, and a life of boundless blessings.

Here are four action steps to help you find joy in your life:

1. Practice Gratitude Daily:

Cultivate a habit of gratitude by taking time each day to reflect on the things you're thankful for. Whether it's the warmth of the sun on your face, a kind word from a friend, or a simple pleasure like your morning coffee, acknowledging these moments of gratitude can shift your focus toward the positive aspects of your life.

2. Mindful Living:

Embrace mindfulness by being fully present in each moment. Engage in activities with your complete attention, whether it's savoring a meal, taking a walk, or having a conversation. By immersing yourself in the present, you'll discover that joy often resides in the little details of life.

3. Nurture Positive Relationships:

Surround yourself with people who uplift and support you. Positive relationships can significantly impact your overall sense of joy. Invest time in nurturing connections with loved ones, engage in meaningful conversations, and offer support to others when they need it. The joy of shared experiences and shared burdens can be profound.

4. Pursue Passions and Hobbies:

Make time for activities and hobbies that bring you genuine happiness. Whether it's painting, playing a musical instrument, gardening, or any other passion, these pursuits can serve as a wellspring of joy. Engaging in activities you love allows you to lose yourself in the moment and experience a deep sense of fulfillment.

Remember that finding joy is an ongoing journey, and it's perfectly normal to have ups and downs. By incorporating these action steps into your daily life, you can gradually shift your perspective and cultivate a greater sense of joy and contentment.

CHOOSE JOY!

Love Nichol

ABOUT AUTHOR
Nichol Perricci

Creative professionals are the driving force of today's business world. Proving to be a quintessential asset in her field; is the multifaceted delineator, Nichol Perricci.

Nichol Perricci is a graphic designer, project manager for group book projects, book publisher, TV/Radio/podcast producer & editor, and content specialist with a high propensity for bringing compassion, ethics, and skill-set diversity to the growing realm of entrepreneurship. Stewarding an array of technical and administrative capabilities, Nichol has spent many years delivering world-class service in project management, social media campaigns, virtual staging, and publishing to a diverse clientele. Her trusted expertise has landed her hand in executive editing for both podcasts and television, by which she resources for a handful of YouTube shows and radio shows each week.

Nichol's mantra is simple: Her goal is to meet clients' standards with unyielding excellence while keeping the integrity of their unique concept and overall brand.

Coupling exceptional work ethic and sincere regard for client satisfaction, Nichol displays an unmatched professional quality that has kept her in high demand for over 20 years. Her current portfolio displays excellence in anthology creation and social media management, proving her uncanny ability to adhere to entrepreneurial trends timelessly. As the Founder of **DNP Presents**, Nichol Perricci remains a reputable help in the creative market, servicing clientele with both complex and simple content needs. She has found her purpose and passion in the publishing industry and her goal is to bring as many stories to the world as possible. She currently serves as the editor and producer of 10+ Radio, Podcast, and YouTube Channels and takes pride in every book she helps write and bring to the world.

Inspired most by those in her field, Nichol longs to aid creative professionals in their pursuit of excellence; helping them to succeed in the fulfillment of their dreams, while living out her own.

NICHOL PERRICCI

When Nichol is not out helping clients and motivating creative entrepreneurs, she is a partner to her husband, Donato, a mother of 3 now grown kiddos, grandma of 2 little peanuts, as well as a pastor's wife, trusted friend, and an asset to her local community.

Nichol Perricci. Innovator. Energizer. Organizer.

Connect with Nichol

https://linktr.ee/nicholperricci

BEAUTIFULLY BROKEN

By Bernice Johnson

My brokenness was God's way of orchestrating my life journey to equip me for a bigger purpose in life. God allowed me to be broken because he knew he would put me back together, new and whole again. Those unique broken pieces during my journey allowed me to find purpose in life. I can now say I live on purpose for a purpose. Oftentimes, we hear others say that they are better today than they were yesterday. I can certainly resonate with that myself. I am truly better today than I was yesterday. Over years, months, weeks, or even days, I was broken and shattered in a million different ways. When life had its way, I became shattered into many pieces and couldn't seem to put those pieces back together. I'm here to share wholeheartedly that we become broken for a breakthrough that manifests the next best version of you.

Who am I? I am her, and she was beautifully broken, which transformed me. I didn't come to share a sob story but to share her story. She is me. You may hear me mention coming from a small country town where my family negatively labeled me, and there were some people I considered friends who criticized me. I wasn't the popular kid in my hometown, and I didn't do much of anything to fit in. A single parent of three, they said I couldn't; God said I could, and I did. As I sit writing this chapter, I can vividly remember how I felt when those negative words were verbally spoken to me that pierced my soul by someone I held near and dear in my heart. Truth be told, I will never be anything more than a low-class country girl and single-parent, and I will never amount to anything in life because my life was completely ruined by the birth of my first son at age 20. The criticism didn't stop there; it became more intense as I became older. I felt like a fish in the sea of deadly sharks. This caused me to take the hurt, the sharp broken pieces, and shame with me into my adulthood, but something major happened in my life in 2020 that shifted my life in a different direction.

This little country girl from Bowman, South Carolina, was seriously scarred, but it took a crisis during a pandemic to clarify my anointing because, for years, I failed to recognize myself and my worth, which led me to push my wants and desires for my children to live a life I failed to live growing up based on the validation of others. So, I fell into the pit of pouring into others' cups to complete them and unknowingly depleting myself. After almost being completely empty, depression struck my family and caught me blind-sighted, and I was totally unprepared to fight a battle that was foreign to me. As a child, I grew up in a home that never spoke of depression or mental health at all. I didn't think any such thing existed. We were told when things got hard in life, to cry it out, let it go, and get back up so we could move on with our lives. So, for me to be struck dealing with my very own child who struggled with a compromised mental health issue was something I was totally uncomfortable with. I had no answer to any questions that arose in my thoughts. Besides, how can I help someone I love battling severe depression when I don't have enough strength to help myself? At that moment, what was I supposed to do? Well, I am glad you asked because I honestly didn't know what to do myself, but I am going to tell you what got me through the darkest times and the hardest moments, especially when destruction shattered my life at the exact moment I decided to take my life back.

Growing up, my mom and granny always taught me that prayer works and that I could always take my prayers and cries to God. I remember that day I got that call about my daughter. I tried mustering up the energy to find my way to my secret place to pray to my heavenly Father because I knew no one could give me what I needed to get through this but him. I walked into my closet and sat on the floor in the dark as I slowly closed the door behind me. As the tears rolled down my face, I simply couldn't get the prayers out verbally, but I remember rocking back and forth, thanking him in advance for giving me the peace that surpasses my own understanding.

Unfortunately, I can't tell you what happened immediately after that because I honestly can't remember myself. However, I can tell you that my flesh kept reminding me that my daughter was still severely depressed and didn't care to live anymore. I rebuked those thoughts because I would and could not accept those thoughts. After praying away those attacks from the enemy, days went by, and I became stronger each day emotionally, physically, and mentally. A lot of what took place after I walked out of that closet is a blur to me. I was surviving, but I wasn't truly living the life God intended for me. As my days and months grew longer, God gave me the spirit of peace and strength that rose inside of me. The spirit of peace and strength allowed me to get through the toughest two years of my life. As we all know, life didn't stop because I was broken and going through my storms. If anything, life seemed more challenging because that storm I was facing had shifted my path into a pathway of uncertainty. I didn't know what to expect next.

A simple ring of my phone would cause my heart to race, and my palms would become sweaty. The thought in the back of my mind was still there when I was contacted as they transported her to the hospital for a suicidal attempt, but I simply had to trust God. Regardless of the path that was designed for me, I embraced it and became suited with the armor of God. I was finally ready to fight. This was now a fight; I knew I was going to win because, by the word of God, my battle was already won.

Two years of my life, which I care not to talk about at times, became something I talk about often because I knew God kept me through it all. Now, I embrace that moment because I can look back to see the goodness of God. It wasn't easy at all, but prayer, fasting, and obedience got me through to the year of 2022.

2022 was a year of transformation for me. I also refer to it as my year of second chances because when I decided to ignite that flickering spark inside of me to a flame that would set the world on fire by telling my story and sharing the glory of God, my entire sense of belonging changed for the better. I am now transforming into the woman that God destined me to be. I had to become the Queen of my jungle and learn to see the forest from the trees.

In life, there will be times when our lights go dim, but it doesn't mean that our lights go completely out. The light is still there; it is just idle and waiting for you to ignite it. Look around and understand that sometimes God uses a storm to clear our pathway to clarify the purpose he has for our lives. As for me, I was pushed into my purpose because that day, depression knocked on my door, and I wasn't ready to answer. It took me on a journey to tell my story to save the lives of many people around the world. In that moment, I fought depleted but not defeated, and it thrust me into an unfamiliar world that allowed me to overcome a major obstacle to be a blessing to others. In 2020, I felt everything was being snatched away from me, but I walked out on faith in 2022. I shared my story of fighting a family crisis that clarified my Godly journey. Since then, I have allowed God to construct my life to pave a pathway for others as I openly share a private part of my world.

In combination with the alignment of God and surrounding myself with people who wanted to see me win, pushing me to greater heights as we positively impact the world. Through it all, I was able to reintroduce that fierce woman that God created me to be. If God did it for me, he will do it for you. I am still here picking up the pieces to create a beautiful picture, and I am still fighting the good fight of faith to build a legacy, advocate for mental health, break those generational curses, build generational wealth, and glorify God because all things are possible when you trust, believe, and depend on him.

So today, I am living my best life while being beautifully broken because I am SHE ~ I am strong, I am Humble, and I am Empowered. Things happen to us that we don't quite understand, but what we fail to realize is that everything happens for a reason: God's reasoning. It happens to add value or clear our path for a divine purpose. I had to believe in myself enough to pull myself away from the critics when some asked why I would tell my personal story about how mental health affected my family, and I looked back at them to ask, *"Why not tell it?"*

I am a walking testimony and a blessing to more people than none. I am not telling my business but telling my story because there is a difference. My story isn't for me to keep to myself but for me to share so that I am able to help someone else. My journey of overcoming by the goodness and mercy of God can be the open umbrella for someone else who may be walking in the rain. God used my journey to glorify his kingdom, and I am being obedient to the will of God and allowing him to transform me to be the best version of me as I help others along the way. My journey wasn't easy, but it was well worth it. I can proudly say that I'm more than a conqueror. It took a crisis in 2020 to snap me out of the unknown world I was residing in.

I was out of alignment with God, so when God allowed his divine intervention to gain access back to my fulfilling life, I devoted myself to reclaiming my life. We don't often get a second chance at anything` let alone life. God gave me a journey of second chances, and I'm not taking it lightly. I'm paving the road to reintroduce myself as the next best version of me. All it took was my very own child to become mentally exhausted, which led to me realizing I was also mentally exhausted. This little small-town country girl ran into a brick wall of mental exhaustion, but by the grace of God, I was able to climb up and jump over that wall by being obedient to the will of God and allowing him to elevate me to limitless possibilities.

So today, I wake up daily to *rise,* which is my moment of gratitude; to *release,* which is my moment to let go of any hindrance; to *renew,* which is my moment of positive thinking; and to *reset* her as she continues to put the pieces back together again. Although, the wall shattered some fragments that were initially broken. I used those same broken pieces to rebuild my lifestyle into a godly masterpiece because I am a piece of the master. I stand once broken but now peacefully placed back together to display a beautiful picture that isn't picture perfect, but it is perfectly mended.

ABOUT AUTHOR
Bernice Johnson

Bernice Johnson is a native of Bowman, South Carolina. She recently gave up the country life to become a resident of the Capital of South Carolina in 2019. She is a certified Life coach and holds licenses in Property & Casualty and Life for South Carolina Department of Insurance. Over 30 years in the insurance industry, Bernice is currently a Senior Commercial Underwriter Assistant, where she supports a team of various commercial property insurance underwriters. Beyond her work responsibilities, Bernice serves as co-chair for personal development for the EmpowerHer ABWA Chapter – Orangeburg, SC. She is an advocate for mental health. She holds an associate degree in business administration. Bernice credits God for her designated journey in which she calls it, a journey of second chances. She believes her storms in life was on purpose to push her into her purpose and thanks God for it all.

Bernice has devoted her life to doing her best to make her past life choices work positively for her and her three children. When depression knocked on her front door and she was afraid to answer, Bernice resolved to work on herself and now uses what she learned from the challenges she faced to help others overcome their obstacles. She has a mindset of a perfectionist, but her life has been far from perfect. Becoming a parent at the young age of 20 years old, and now as a single mother of three, Bernice realized that she had to work on herself and build a life for her family. She developed the F.O.Y.E.R. method and has found great success in turning negative situations into positive learning opportunities for growth. F.O.Y.E.R. is an acronym for Focus On Yourself Every day Regardless.

In 2023, Bernice became an award-winning and bestselling author of Keep on Keeping on: Your G.R.O.W.T.H Will Bear Fruit to Feed Others. She is a 3x collaborating author of three bestselling anthologies, The Champion Mindset, More Than a Conqueror and Igniting the Millionaire: Become Her to be Her. Bernice has been spotlighted in the Women of Purpose

& Dignity Magazine. She was awarded as Brand Ambassador for the Hoinser Group and recognized as one of the Top 100 Inspirational Women in Hoinser Group Queens Magazine in 2022.

Acknowledging and recognizing that feeling of hopelessness that so often causes people to get stuck, Bernice seeks to be an inspiration to others and give them hope. She has overcome many trials and tribulations in her own life and wants to show people that they can conquer even the most difficult situations they may have encountered. She is a recovering workaholic but has since slowed down to stop and smell the roses. When she is not helping others, Bernice finds great fulfillment in daily journaling.

Connect with Bernice:

Email: Johnsonbernice829@gmail.com
Instagram: authorbernicejohnson
Facebook: Bernice Johnson & Bernice Johnson, Author

A STAR WAS BORN
EMBRACING
SELF-DISCOVERY
By Dalia Ganzel

As we navigate the journey of life, there comes a key moment when we embark on a profound journey to truly know ourselves. It transcends the superficial knowledge of our name, gender, titles, occupation, place of residence, or marital status. It delves into the essence of who we are, our values, traits, interests, and ultimate purpose in life.

Self-discovery involves research and begins with a wish: Does God really bring us joy and fulfillment? It involves understanding the difference between our personality - shaped by external influences - and our authentic self. Who do we like to hang out with? What activities ignite a sense of passion within us? What makes us really happy? And in the service of what noble purpose are we here?

This journey is an opportunity to peel back layers and reveal the unique qualities that make us who we are at our core. This requires introspection and reflection as we unravel the intricacies of our being. By distinguishing between societal expectations and our true desires, we can align with what resonates deep within us. This process allows us to embrace our individuality without hesitation or apology.

As you embark on this path of self-discovery, remember that it is an ongoing exploration that evolves alongside your growth as an individual. Embrace each revelation as a stepping-stone towards an authentic life. Discovering your true self empowers you to live in alignment with your values and passions while making a meaningful contribution to the lives of others. By fully understanding yourself - beyond external labels - you unlock unlimited potential for personal growth and fulfillment. Embrace this transformative journey with curiosity and openness; let it guide you to a life full of authenticity, purposeful connections, and true happiness.

I encourage you now as you read these words: take time for introspection and self-reflection. Explore your values and passions; Embrace your unique qualities without hesitation or apology. Discover what brings you joy and how you can use those gifts to improve others. You were born with a purpose, and as you continue to get to know yourself better, you will find new ways to share your blessings with the world. Embrace this beautiful journey of self-discovery and let it guide you toward a life filled with love, meaning, and service. A star was born inside you a long time ago - now is the time to let it shine brightly for all to see.

Here are some practical suggestions to help you in self-discovery, introspection, and exploring your unique values, passions, and qualities:

1. **Create a quiet space**: Find a peaceful environment where you can have uninterrupted time for reflection. It could be a cozy corner in your home or a serene spot in nature.

2. **Journaling**: Start keeping a journal to record your thoughts, feelings, and experiences. Write freely without judgment or censorship. Use prompts like "What brings me joy?" or "What are my core values?" to guide your reflections.

3. **Mindfulness and meditation**: Practice mindfulness techniques or meditation to cultivate present-moment awareness and connect with your inner self. This can help you gain clarity about what truly matters to you.

4. **Seek solitude**: Set aside regular periods of solitude where you can disconnect from distractions and spend quality time alone with yourself. Use this time for introspection and deep thinking.

5. **Engage in creative activities**: Explore different forms of creative expression, such as painting, writing, dancing, or playing an instrument. These activities can unlock hidden passions within you and provide insights into who you are at the core.

6. **Seek new experiences**: Step out of your comfort zone by trying new things that pique your interest but may be unfamiliar to you. This could involve taking up a new hobby or participating in workshops related to subjects that intrigue you.

7. **Reflect on past experiences**: Take time to reflect on significant moments from your past - both positive and challenging ones - as they often hold valuable lessons about yourself and what truly matters to you.

8. **Connect with others who inspire you**: Surround yourself with people who embody qualities that resonate with the person you aspire to become or who share similar interests as yours; their energy can ignite inspiration within yourself.

9. **Practice self-care routines**: Engage in activities that nurture your physical, mental, and emotional well-being regularly – exercise regularly, get enough sleep, eat nutritious food, and engage in activities that bring you joy.

10. **Volunteer or help others**: Engaging in acts of service can provide a sense of purpose and fulfillment. Look for opportunities to use your unique gifts and talents to make a positive impact on the lives of others.

BE YOUR FUTURE SELF NOW

Remember, self-discovery is a lifelong journey. Be patient with yourself and allow the process to unfold naturally.

Embrace each step along the way as an opportunity for growth and self-understanding. You have within you all that is needed to uncover your true essence and make a meaningful difference in the world!

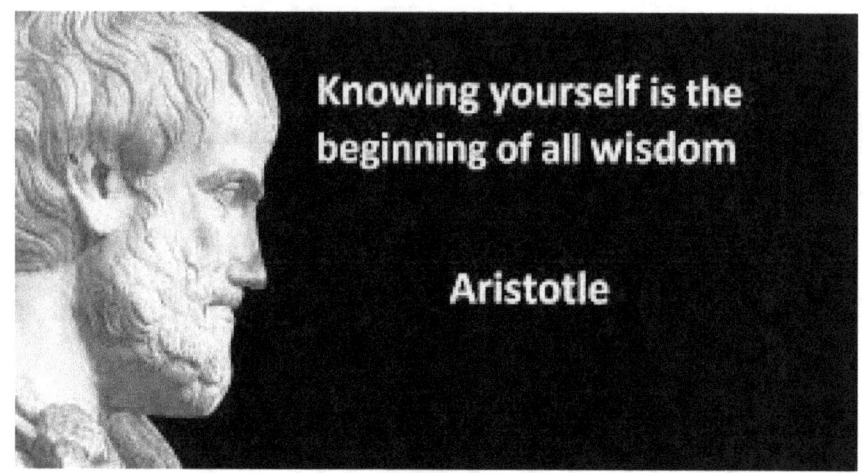

How to Create Your Next Best Version?

Reignite Your Life and Constantly Renew

Here, we will explore the importance of constantly renewing and igniting the flame in all aspects of your life. By understanding the significance of ongoing growth and development, you can ensure that you are always challenged, growing, staying relevant, and leading a fascinating life journey.

Life is an ever-evolving process that requires constant change and exploration. Embracing this understanding allows you to reinvent yourself continually and move forward into the next phase of your life. It's about asking yourself, "What's next for me?"

The Freedom to Change

Adopting a mindset focused on creating your next best version is truly captivating. It grants you the freedom to be open-minded, creative, adaptable, and willing to change. By embracing this mindset, you become open to infinite possibilities while reshaping your life as you progress.

Embrace Change as an Opportunity for Growth

Change can be intimidating or uncomfortable for many people; however, when viewed through the lens of personal growth and self-improvement, it becomes an exciting opportunity. Embrace change as a catalyst for transformation rather than something to fear or resist.

Constantly Seek New Experiences

To create your next best version requires actively seeking new experiences that challenge you mentally, emotionally, or physically. Step out of your comfort zone regularly by trying new things – whether it's learning a new skill or exploring unfamiliar territories – these experiences will expand your horizons and contribute to personal growth.

Keep Learning to Evolve and Grow

Never stop learning! Cultivate a thirst for knowledge by engaging in lifelong learning opportunities such as reading books on various subjects or attending workshops/seminars related to areas that interest you. This commitment to continuous learning ensures that you are always evolving into a better version of yourself.

Surround Yourself with Inspiring Individuals

The company we keep greatly influences our personal growth. Surround yourself with individuals who inspire and challenge you to become your best self. Seek out mentors, coaches, or like-minded individuals who can support and guide you on your journey of self-improvement.

Embrace Resilience and Adaptability

Life is full of unexpected twists and turns. Embracing resilience and adaptability allows you to navigate through challenges with grace and determination. Remember that setbacks are opportunities for growth, and each obstacle presents a chance to learn valuable lessons about yourself.

Celebrate Your Progress

Acknowledge the progress you make along the way as you create your next best version. Celebrate even the smallest victories, as they are stepping-stones towards becoming the person you aspire to be.

In this chapter, we have explored how embracing constant renewal, change, exploration, open-mindedness, learning, resilience, and adaptability can help create your next best version. By adopting these principles into your life journey, you will continue to evolve into an even more extraordinary individual while living a fulfilling life filled with endless possibilities.

Harnessing the Power of Higher Guidance

Let's explore the profound impact of incorporating a higher power into your life journey. Whether you believe in God, your spirit, or your higher self, developing a relationship with this guiding force can provide invaluable support and guidance as you strive to become your next best version.

Recognizing the Presence of Higher Guidance

Acknowledge that there is a greater force at work in the universe. This force is available to assist and guide you on your path toward personal growth and self-discovery. By opening yourself up to this presence, you invite its wisdom and guidance into your life.

Cultivating a Relationship with Your Guidance

Take time to develop a deep connection with your higher power. This can be done through prayer, meditation, or any practice that allows you to quiet your mind and connect with something beyond yourself. Nurture this relationship by regularly seeking guidance and expressing gratitude for the support received.

Asking for Guidance and Support

Don't hesitate to ask for assistance from your higher power when faced with challenges or uncertainties. Trust that by reaching out for guidance, answers will be revealed in due time. Be specific in what you seek assistance with and remain open-minded about how it may manifest.

Being Open to Receive

Maintain an open heart and mind as you await signs or messages from your higher power. These messages may come through intuitive feelings, synchronicities in daily life, or even insights gained during moments of reflection. Be receptive to these subtle cues as they guide you towards making choices aligned with becoming your next best version.

Transcending Illusions of Reality

The illusion of reality often distracts us from our true purpose and potential. By connecting with a higher power, we gain clarity amidst the chaos of everyday life. This connection helps us see beyond surface-level concerns and aligns us with our deeper values and aspirations.

Finding Ease and Grace on Your Journey

When you invite your higher power into your life journey, you tap into a wellspring of ease and grace. Trust that the guidance received will lead you towards the path of least resistance, allowing for smoother transitions and a sense of flow. Embrace this support as it helps navigate challenges with greater resilience and peace.

Embracing Faith in the Unknown

As you embark on your journey towards becoming your next best version, embrace faith in the unknown. Trust that your higher power has a plan for you, even if it may not be immediately clear. Surrender control over outcomes and have faith that everything is unfolding as it should.

By incorporating a higher power into your life journey, you access an infinite source of wisdom, love, and guidance. This connection provides solace during times of uncertainty while propelling you forward on the path to self-discovery with grace and ease. Embrace this relationship wholeheartedly as it supports your transformation into an extraordinary version of yourself.

ASK YOURSELF, WHAT'S NEXT FOR ME?

How you might know it's time for a change in your life. Here are a few questions to ask yourself:

1. Are you feeling stagnant or unfulfilled? If you find yourself lacking motivation or a sense of purpose in your current situation, it may be a sign that it's time for a change.

2. Do you feel disconnected from your values and passions? If your current path no longer aligns with what truly matters to you, it could be an indication that it's time to explore new opportunities.

3. Are you constantly yearning for something more? If there is a persistent longing for growth and new experiences, it might be an indication that change is necessary to fulfill those desires.

4. Have external circumstances shifted significantly? Life events such as job loss, relationship changes, or personal growth can often signal the need for change and adaptation.

5. Are you experiencing negative effects on your mental or physical well-being? If your current situation is causing stress, anxiety, burnout, or other detrimental effects on your health and well-being, it may be time to consider making changes that prioritize self-care.

Remember that everyone's journey is unique and individual circumstances vary greatly. Trusting your intuition and listening to what feels right for you will ultimately guide you towards recognizing when it's time for a change in your life path.

Asking "**What's next?**" signifies a profound understanding of the game of life, which is constantly evolving and requires continuous personal growth. It suggests a readiness for the next challenge, a determination to achieve one's highest potential, and an unwavering commitment to living purposefully and passionately. Trusting one's inner guidance to guide the way and allowing music to inspire a deeply meaningful life, one can create a masterpiece of their next best self.

Please do not hesitate to send me a message if you are interested in gaining insights into my personal story, I would be delighted to share it with you.

I cordially invite you to stay connected by scanning the QR Code located below. By doing so, you will gain access to valuable information that may assist you in achieving your success goals.

Let's Stay Connected: https://beacons.ai/ganzelmentoring

ABOUT AUTHOR
Dalia Ganzel

Dalia Ganzel is a dynamic and visionary leader known for her wisdom, insights for self-realization and creative leadership skills. As a founder of Ganzel Mentoring, she empowers business entrepreneurs and teams to achieve unprecedented success using their superpowers.

With over two decades of coaching small businesses, entrepreneurs, and teams, she encourages free thinking, creativity, and non-conformism as a way of life in a society that long lost its path, she promotes personal leadership and responsibility to inspire, empower and provoke hope. Dalia also helped countless people to find their calling, their unique tone, reach their personal and accomplish their personal and professional goals through innovative leadership.

She never misses an opportunity to voice her opinion, challenges the audience to free thinking through essential questions, Dalia is an authority and certified in life coaching, business consulting and the developer of the program: "Empowering Through Creativity. Her altruistic nature extends beyond her work, as an active contributor to the community while expending substantive ties with loved ones and colleagues.

"Creativity is intelligence having fun."
~ Albert Einstein

Her flagship program, "Empowering Through Creativity": Unlocking Leadership Mastery, has become a global movement promoting change that is exponentially intensifying, since each member becomes a beacon of influence that lights the way to their circles of influence. We need a critical mass to bring the desired change to humanity at these critical times.

Connect with Dalia

Website: www.ganzelmentoring.com
Email: ganzelmentoring@gmail.com
Social-Media: https://beacons.ai/ganzelmentoring

DAMAGED RE-BRANDED

By Mildred Etherton

A buse is a shattering experience that can have a catastrophic impact on one's life. In this chapter, I will share my story of how my abuse changed my life. My hope is that my story will inspire and motivate those who have experienced similar traumas, and help them find the strength and resilience to live life to the fullest.

THE BEGINNING

When I was about four years old, I was removed from my home and taken for a ride in a police car to what would become my *"new foster home."* The reason for being removed was due to the sexual abuse I was experiencing along with physical. After we arrived and got inside the officer and our "foster mom" chatted. When the officer left, I remember my foster mom running a shower. I was in a bathroom that appeared dark to me. She went to undress me and I remember the tears coming out of my eyes as a sling came off my arm. As I got in the shower, I was trying to understand why I even had to take a shower when I first arrived. Was I dirty? Was this just part of how things were done? Why am I in what is called Pajama's? Why did I not get to bring anything from my home with me? I thought a lot about my mother, father, and other siblings.

I just met an entire new family that was mixed with a foster mom, and other children. Am I going to be safe here? Who is going to tuck me in at night? How long do I have to stay here for? Is this going to be my forever home now? I already have a mom, but now I have two mommy's. That night after seeing our room which was way bigger than where we were living, my sister was fast asleep. Once she went to sleep, I let my tears flow laying there alone, while I held my pillow very tightly until I fell asleep myself.

A few years went on and we were able to see our other siblings and visitations with my dad. Somewhere in this shuffle at age 7, my dad got custody of us again. At this time, we went for another very long car ride with him and all my siblings. I had a new baby brother at this time. We then get to what is now our new home. I have another new mommy, my four younger siblings, and now 3 more siblings to make a total of 8 of us children. The excitement of just being together, a family again really made me happy. I did not think about all the horrible things I had gone through previously. I did not think about my birth mother at all in this moment. I was just happy to be able to protect my siblings and be a happy family.

Little did I know, that the addictions, the physical, sexual, and emotional abuse would become something that was normalized in our home yet again! At the age of 13 we were placed back into states care and separated. As a teenager in the system and moving around from placement to placement with nothing more than memories or a garbage bag full of items, and eventually *"aging out of the system"* at 18 years old made it difficult to find my place in the world. There I was 18 years old, finally free, excited, and overwhelmed all at the same time with no family trying to figure out how to survive in the world alone!

MY LEARNED BELIEFS

Un-worthy, not wanted, un-loved, damaged, I do not need you, and good girl were all the labels I had branded myself with on my heart for several years. Since I was removed from my family, I stayed in that survival mode of "being the good girl." I had already learned that from a young age, "If I just stayed focused on school, got good grades, and did not get in any trouble, I would not be questioned by anyone, and maybe someone would want and love me." Being removed at a young age made me feel like I was not wanted. I did not understand what was happening. Removed again as a teenager, you start to miss what you had at home no matter how bad it was, because being shuffled around from placement to placement hurts you more on a deeper level and you begin to feel as if everything you do is wrong and your fault. I truly believed that no one wanted me because I was damaged, a bad person, and not worthy of family.

STEPS TO REBRANDING:

Dedicate time to prayer, meditation, and being still. Your time is *"new"* shine!

At about 7 or 8 years old I was able to go to church with my neighbor. I remember doing the alter call and accepting Christ in my heart. At this age, I did not understand what was happening and all I remember is feeling so safe and loved in that moment. I knew who Christ was and I knew I could pray to him and he would hear everything I said. There where many nights I would lay in my bed crying and praying that God will make my parents change. I never understood why we as kids were forced to go to church every Sunday while my parents stayed home. As I got older and grew in my faith, I realized looking back that there was no way I could have survived the many things I went through if there was no God. Getting rest, meditating, clearing you mind and being still will allow you to hear clearly and give you an opportunity to be polished to shine!

*A*ffirm yourself!

I know we hear this all the time from people. Self-affirmations. Weird right? The first time I went the therapy as an adult this was stressed to me. I had all these negative beliefs about myself. You know when you go to a job interview, and they ask you what your strengths are? I remember at one point in my life I could not name a single strength of mine, yet there are so many. When we start to believe the lies that we make up about ourselves, it is so hard to see anything positive about who we are. We doubt everything we do and thus in return causes us to go to very lonely places. When I read scripture, I believe all those things that God says about me. So, go ahead and be your biggest cheerleader. The more you say it to yourself, the more you believe in yourself. I learned how to be kind and gentle to ME by practicing daily.

*M*aintain and own your truth... Shame is not my name!

The truth is, *"I was completely broken and lost. I was hurting. I knew I would never have my siblings with me and I was beyond crushed."* I would often think about what I could have done different to protect them. My abuser who identified himself as my dad, told me for many years, if I ever told anyone what was going on I would never have a family again. I'll never forget the forensic interview at 13 years old, when the initial removal happened the second time. I personally had nothing to say. I knew that if I said anything at all, the hope of being a family would be gone and not to mention, I did not know if I was going back home with my abuser so I was terrified of what would happen next. Going to school I was labeled the *"group home girl."* Having that label hurt me. It was a constant reminder of how I was worthless and I was never good enough. When I was about 30 I decided to get court records to read things. This bought on more shame and guilt. When I realized that my abuser was not sentenced for everything it brought me to a very low place where I wanted to give up on life. Some time went on and I realized I was doing the very same thing to myself others where doing. I was branding myself. Sure, I was not another statistic, but I was devaluing my worth of who I really was. One day, I remember sitting praying and reading the bible. It was spoken very clearly to me that I was worthy. That I did not need to ever be ashamed of who I was because God is not ashamed of me. In fact, he loves me just the way I am. In that God moment, I decided that I no longer was going to continue to hold onto the label of shame. I decided to hold onto my worth instead and when I would start to doubt who I was, I would just remind myself the very words that were spoken to me, *"Shame is not my name."* I know now that my past is part of who I am, but it is also part of why I am here!!!!!

*A*ssume nothing! My thoughts are not always the truth...

How often have we been somewhere and someone looks at you and you think, *"Did I do something?"* How about when we have seen something happening and you just wonder what in the world is going on? For many years, I lived in my head. I naturally am a processor and take time to think about things. I also am an observer. There was a season I went through for about a year. My very near and dear Pastor challenged me. I sat down with him and had a conversation. See, the problem I had is I would make up the beliefs about my interactions with people whether something was said or not said and turn it into something unreal. He asked me when I was at church and starting with him to ask very clear specific questions to whatever that interaction may have been. I started to realize that peoples' reactions, smiles, looks, conversations, ect were not always ill intended. I learned that by living in my head I was not only criticizing myself, but I was doing it to others. By asking clarifying questions I learned to not become attached to the responses from others. This allowed me to practice giving myself and other people grace while understanding what other's intentions are.

*G*et out of contentment lane!

Living outside your contentment lane means doing things that you would not normally do or taking risks that you would not typically take. It's about pushing yourself to try new things or face challenging situations that make you feel uncomfortable or uncertain. You might experience fear, anxiety, or even failure, but stepping outside your contentment lane can also be incredibly rewarding. Living outside your contentment lane is essential for personal growth and development. When you step out, you challenge yourself to learn new skills, develop new perspectives, and embrace new experiences. It can help you overcome fear and build confidence, develop resilience, and cultivate a sense of adventure and exploration. You break out of old patterns and habits that may be limiting your potential. It allows you to tap into your creative side and explore new ways of thinking, problem-solving, and adapting to change. Here I am, way uncomfortable, sharing my story in hopes to create change!

*E*ngage and connect meaningful with others without expectation!!

Despite the inter dialogue I would have with myself, I always wondered who *"I"* was. There were many nights and days I just wish someone could see pass the *"good girl"* and say to me *"I see you hurting."* To be completely honest, if someone was to even ask me how I was doing, more than likely I would lie to them and say, *"I am good."* No one was a constant in my life. I had this attitude I do not need anyone! I was not going to let anyone see me for who I was. I was so scared that if someone really knew the hurt they would just feel sorry for me and or, I would be labeled more, not to mention that I would try to share things with a therapist I had and often would be told, *"You are deflecting or minimizing your feelings."* I became so good at making people think I was ok and fine. Last thing I wanted was to be a zombie from medications, not to mention, I would hear lots of conversations about others in my homes and how they get more money for people with diagnosis. I made up my mind that I was not going to ever be diagnosed or a reason for someone to gain more money because of my label or diagnosis. As time went on in life, I realized this attitude just made me lonelier and I would live isolated. I would do everything I could to hurt and push other people away unintentionally. It was my way of protecting myself. I started to let go of the expectations I had and started to let people love on me. I would enjoy those moments and either those people would stay and or not stay. I had this epiphany that, people will come and go in your life for seasons and reason's. I slowly became un attached to the need of wanting what I thought was normal. I slowly let go of all the bad things that happened to me and held onto the good times and the good memories. Human connection has improved my life!

Dream it and attempt it!

Each one of us has a story and though maybe we may have walked the journey together in some way, shape or form, it is important to remember that our experiences may be different and is seen through a different lens. You see, healing is a journey. There should never be a time line put on how long it will take. As I shed all the different layers of trauma I have been through, I become a stronger and better person. Every single person on this earth has an opinion. Some people are never afraid to just let you know what they think of you. I encourage you to not brand yourself with a hot iron. Yes, labels and diagnosis may be part of what other people say we are, but they do not debilitate me. As I continue to heal, let people in my life, share my story, embrace my flaws, I stay confident with who I am. I am not a product of what happened to me or what people have said I am. I am not another statistic. I simply am a beautiful, loving, honest and humble, person who as many scars and knows, I am worthy, loved, and God's most desired treasure. Without hope, faith, or vision, we stay stuck from igniting our absolute loving best self to ourselves and others.

CHALLENGE...

I know what it is like to feel like you are totally alone and that no one would understand you. The hurt we feel from people when we have trauma causes some deep wounds that we often don't want to re-open. I promise they can heal. I get it. I would much rather live in my shell by myself, however, this causes me to live lonely, and to go to dark places in my mind. Keep learning and growing. Embrace a lifelong journey of personal/spiritual growth and self-improvement. Seek knowledge and wisdom, challenge yourself, talk or listen to someone with intent, practice gratitude, and embrace new opportunities knowing we may get hurt in the process. I am going where my heart takes me wholeheartedly without expectation! You and I matter. We are loved and we have purpose! Let us live it out! Please join me in creating positive legacy change...

ABOUT AUTHOR
Mildred Etherton

Meet Millie, an extraordinary individual whose life has been an inspiring journey of service and compassion. Hailing from the heart of Arizona, Mildred Etherton, affectionately known as Millie, overcame tremendous odds from an early age. Spending a decade as a ward of the state, she faced challenges head-on until she reached the age of 18, when she gracefully aged out of care.

Millie's determination and love for helping others led her to pursue a bachelor's degree in human services, setting the foundation for her remarkable career. She successfully runs a business with her husband, all while cherishing a beautiful marriage that has flourished for 17 years, having found her high school sweetheart. Their love has blessed them with four wonderful children, bringing immeasurable joy to their lives.

Throughout her youth and into adulthood, Millie has been a fierce advocate for youth in care, dedicating her time and efforts to empower and support those facing similar challenges she once endured. Her professional journey has been deeply rooted in working with children and families with behavioral health needs, enriching lives, and spreading hope wherever she goes.

With an unwavering faith in the Lord, Millie finds solace and inspiration. Her creative spirit finds expression in writing and music, and she delights in the wonders of the great outdoors, enjoying activities such as hunting, camping, laughing, and cooking. But above all, she treasures the moments spent making memories with her cherished family.

A true embodiment of selflessness, Millie's passion lies in serving others, wholeheartedly embracing the diversity of needs and obstacles they may encounter. From a place of genuine humility, she shares her powerful stories, hoping to inspire and ignite positive change wherever it is needed.

Millie's life is a testament to the incredible gifts of service and empathy she possesses. Her journey continues to inspire and uplift those fortunate enough to cross paths with this remarkable individual.

"I will not leave you as orphans: I will come to you. Before long, the world will not see me anymore, but you will see me. Because I live, you also will live."

John 14:18-19

Connect with Millie

123etherton@gmail.com

FB millie.seehofferetherton

CATAPULTED TO GREATNESS (UNMERITED FAVOUR)
By Joyce Kamau

Beyond Imagination

"No eye has seen, no ear has heard, no mind has conceived what God has prepared for those who love Him." *1 Corinthians 2:9*

Focus all your attention on God with the understanding that His ways and His thoughts are greater than you can ever imagine.

Be ready to embrace greatness and overflowing blessings with humility and grace.

A Determined Little Village Girl

Growing up in the rural Kenyan highlands, I had big dreams; I had no doubt in my mind that I would be successful in the future and help my family. I had to! It was important for me to uplift my family. However, I never imagined that my cup would overflow. As a little village girl, I did chores, often going to fetch water from river *Gathigi* and fetch firewood from the nearby forest with the support of the mothers in the neighbourhood who were experts in tying the firewood securely for transportation using donkeys. Growing up was fun. During the weekends, with my sisters, cousins, and friends, like Ruth in the Bible, we embarked on an exciting adventure of gathering wheat grain left behind by combine harvesters from the large wheat fields owned by the wealthy farmers. Our mothers would then make delicious homemade bread known as *mikondi chapati* from the wheat flour.

My parents were peasant farmers with a medium-sized farm. My mother kept two dairy cows and grew food crops: potatoes, peas, beans, carrots, kale, cabbage, and maize/corn. These were for food; however, any surplus would be sold to meet family financial obligations. I helped my mother sell her farm produce in the local farmers market. This was exciting as I always got a treat - mouth-watering samosas at Maina Gathege's restaurant.

The milk would serve the family. My mother sold the surplus to the Molo Dairy Farmers, where she served as a member of the Molo Dairy Board. A portion of the farm was dedicated to pyrethrum, a cash crop that was lucrative at the time. I detested picking pyrethrum flowers, especially during the dry season, as the dry stems would really prick hard.

I walked a six-kilometre journey to my primary school with no shoes and often in the biting Molo morning dew. School mornings were challenging. However, the return journey home in the afternoon was fun. We played along the way and enjoyed eating wild fruits, mainly raspberries and gooseberries, quenching our thirst with the pure spring waters of the Molo meadows. I had a fantastic and memorable childhood.

While schooling at the little-known Kambala primary school in Molo, I showed up at an early age, linking up with two other girls who became incredibly good friends to showcase musical performances during special days at school. Lydia had moved from Nairobi City to live with her grandmother in Molo. Wendy had relocated to Kenya from the United States of America with her missionary parents, who joined the teaching team at our school. Magìrì (as I was known then), the village girl, did not shy away from teaming up with the two girls to make a powerful trio. I did not feel intimidated by their exposure in big cities; I was my true self, eager to learn and embrace the opportunity to be the best I could be. We made great performances, winning accolades from teachers, parents, and fellow students. I was brilliant in my academics, too, usually taking the first, second, or third positions, which I would rotate between myself and two boys in my class. Notwithstanding the challenges of schooling as a little girl in Molo, I excelled in the national primary exam. I proceeded to Naivasha Girls High School and later to State House Girls School in Nairobi, Kenya, a prestigious school in the neighbourhood of State House Nairobi - the official residence of the president of Kenya, for my "*A*" Levels on attaining a first division in the national secondary exam! At State House Girls, I honed my leadership skills, becoming a Deputy House Captain for Simba House. No mean achievement for a rural girl!

Looking back to my childhood through schooling and my career journey, working in the international arena, I can attest that, indeed, if you humble yourselves under the mighty hand of God, that He will exalt you in due time. It does not matter where you come from or the challenges you might have faced growing up; our destiny is always in God's hands.

Nourishing Your Mind

Mind food - Wisdom or weed?

"Whatever is true, whatever is noble, whatever is right, whatever is pure, whatever is lovely, whatever is admirable - if anything is excellent or praiseworthy - think about such things."

Philippians 4:8.

Focus on the things that are pleasing to God. Be of high moral principles, promoting ethical practices and doing right. Set a good example as a person of good repute. Be authentic, bearing in mind that your name is your value. Feed your mind with the right stuff. Think positively and remove unwanted, negative thoughts from your mind. Ensure that there is no room in your mind for limiting beliefs and self-doubt. Things that hold you back. Identify what holds you back and let it go because you can do everything through Christ, who gives you strength (Philippians 4:13).

My prayer is that God creates in me a clean and pure heart and renews the right spirit within me so that I may worship Him.

Embrace change, being flexible with the ability to adapt to new environments and situations. Change brings new challenges and opportunities with the potential to reveal the absolute best in us. Be intentional with everything you do, embracing a growth mindset that demonstrates determination, discipline, and consistency. Maintain high standards no matter the situation. Do not compromise your integrity and showcase resilience in the face of adversity. Display a can-do attitude self-drive with passion, great energy, and enthusiasm to see you through the storm. Remain resilient and do not quit, no matter the challenges. *"Consider it pure joy, my brothers and sisters, whenever you face trials of many kinds, because you know that the testing of your faith produces perseverance "* James 1:2-3. It is not easy to celebrate tough times. However, if there is ever a time when you must be brave, audacious, tenacious, persistent, determined, and innovative, it is through the storms of life. Never ever give up.

Pursue your dream no matter the circumstances. You can be all you want to be. You deserve it! You are worthy of greatness!

Lessons from my mother

In a short month, it will be ten years, a decade, since my beloved mother's promotion to glory in October 2013. Losing my mother was the most devastating experience in my life. My mum was my rock, the epitome of wisdom!

Growing up in a rural setting under the wings of my mother, I learnt pretty early the importance of showing up with courage and determination. My beloved mother *(Nyina wa Karimi)* did not go to school; however, she was the first woman and resourceful member of the Molo Dairy Board in the late eighties and early nineties, a dedicated Church Deacon, and a member of the Women's guild at the Molo Presbyterian Church. In her later years, she was also the Patron of the Sunday school at Munju Presbyterian Church, a branch of the main Molo Presbyterian Church. My mother worked extremely hard as a small-scale farmer to raise eight of us while my dad worked in the city. She woke up early to milk her cows in time for the early morning milk collections and prepared our snacks for school, including the yummy charcoal-roasted corn. It was remarkable how she balanced all her responsibilities successfully and without complaints. She had a big heart and was a cheerful giver, always sharing whatever she had with the less fortunate in the village.

She valued education and could not bow to pressure from other parents in the community to move me to a new school in the neighborhood that would ease my long, chilly journey to school but make me repeat a year of school. She was determined to see my progress without any disruptions; she believed in me and had no doubt that I would cope and excel.

Meeting Masterclass - A Mother's Wisdom

As a member of the Molo Dairy Board, my mother gained exposure to formal and structured conduct of meetings. This was a skill she was keen to share and inculcate in the various community gatherings. It was normal for us to hear her mention standard meeting terminologies often with a Kikuyu accent, such as: agenda *"ajeda,"* matters arising *"mataraisini,"* minutes *"mīnīti"* Any Other Business (AOB) *"obi."* She emphasised the power of showing up and making your voice heard. Through her tenacity, she travelled across the country for conferences and agriculture trade fairs. I vividly remember her travels to Embu and Naivasha as she would share her lived experiences and how she made her voice heard. This was truly inspiring for me at an early age. She taught me the value of hard work, determination, courage, tenacity, speaking up, perseverance, conflict resolution, and strong faith in God. Her favorite verses, Philippians 4:4-5,

"Rejoice in the Lord always, I will say it again Rejoice! Let your gentleness be evident to all. The LORD is near."

Her conflict resolution reference was guided by the beatitudes: "Blessed are the peacemakers for they will be called sons of God" Matthew 5:9. She was the embodiment of servant leadership. I'm so blessed to have had *Nyina wa Karimi* as my mother. I'm forever grateful to God for her life and the memories we hold, and above all that, my mother taught us the value of having a relationship with God. God bless her soul. May she rest in eternal repose till we meet again in the heavenly places.

Lessons from my Father

My dad left us to be with the Lord four years after my mother's promotion to glory. He taught me loyalty, diligence, sacrifice, and giving with a cheerful heart. He was the firstborn in my grandmother's family. Belonging to the wider clan, he held his siblings' hands and those of his many cousins. He gave generously, even his own clothing! He valued education and was determined to give all his children an opportunity for the best possible education that he could afford.

Trusted hands

My dad was a trusted and loyal chauffeur of thirty years for the General Managers at Olympic Airways, the Greek airline regional offices in Nairobi, Kenya. He worked diligently and won the confidence of his bosses, who changed every five years. Through his dedication and loyalty, one of his bosses entrusted him to travel with his children for summer holiday to his home country, Corfu, Greece.

Determination and courage were strong foundations in his driving career. I recall him sharing his experience while taking his driving test under the strict supervision of the colonial police/driving supervisor. He was the only one who attained the pass mark in a group of about twenty candidates. He recalled with satisfaction how the strict supervisor was impressed by how my dad navigated the steep and curved route in the upper hill area of Nairobi city. The strict driving supervisor did not intimidate my dad. He was determined to excel.

My dad was the most generous human being. Whenever he visited us in the village in Molo, he would bring sweets and biscuits for all the children in the village! He was the most loving father. He would buy me and my two younger sisters, Wanjiru and Wangui, matching dresses, shoes, combs, and umbrellas, among others. Whenever we visited him in the city during the school holidays, he would take us on city tours. The Nairobi animal orphanage was an unforgettable experience. He bought us treats; the most memorable was the Lyons Maid Ice Cream! He was an amazing father. God bless his soul.

I was truly inspired by the values instilled in us by my parents. Even though they are not physically with us today, I feel their presence every day. May they both rest in tranquillity.

Elevated: Visualising Greatness

Enjoy the view from the top. Visualise your greatness, enjoying every sight, sound, feel, smell, and taste of your success. Emotionally connect with the picture of your success, having a vivid description in your mind that produces powerful feelings with clear images in the mind that drive you towards pursuing your greatness.

Steve Jobs once said, *"If you are working on something you really care about, you don't have to be pushed. The vision pulls you. Therefore, remain focused on your desired destination. Keep your eyes on the goal."* Proverbs 4:25 reminds us that we should let our eyes look straight ahead, fixing our gaze directly before us. Do not be swayed or distracted, don't allow excuses to creep in. Speak blessing upon your life—the power of Faith. With God, nothing is impossible. Keep the faith, don't get talked out of your dreams. Our God is an awesome God. He fulfils the desires of our hearts.

Build and enhance your value by learning, unlearning, and relearning. Advance yourself, raise your bar, and maintain high standards. Gain new skills and knowledge to propel you to greatness. Become the best version of you!

Do not wait for an opportunity to present itself; create it yourself. Many people are hurting. Seize the opportunity and have positive influence in people's lives. This brings meaning to your goal. Sustain this by sharing skills and knowledge. Sharing is caring. Uplift others. Hold their hands, transforming lives from your Jerusalem to Judea, Samaria and beyond.

My cup overflows

Exceedingly; Abundantly; Bountiful; Overflowing, and immeasurable with peace, joy, and gratitude. The Almighty God is the God of overflow. He is mighty and able to surpass our requests and thoughts. He is Jehovah Jireh; God is our provider. He is El Shaddai - our God of more than enough. He is able to do exceedingly abundantly above all that we ask or think.

I can attest that; indeed, God prepares a table before me in the presence of my enemies. He anoints my head with oil; my cup overflows (Psalm 23:5). What was meant for my harm, God changed the evil plans of the enemy to a reason for His glory. Throughout my career, I have faced numerous challenges - friends turned foes, betrayal, humiliation, and more. I was emotionally depleted. It was a tough place to be in. I was in the valley. I could have easily given up. However, it has never been lost on me that the dream is HUGE! It's beyond me. It's about making a difference. The bigger the dream, the bigger the obstacles.

The storms did not overwhelm me. God upheld me with His mighty hand.

The joy of the Lord is always my strength. The stronger the storm, the bigger the blessings that lie ahead of you. All we need to do is to commit ourselves to being the best we can be at all times. While in the valley, keep the faith and believe in the possibilities. Take comfort in knowing that God's power is made perfect in weakness. The Bible reminds us that those who hope in the Lord will renew their strength. They will soar on wings like eagles; they will run and not grow weary; they will walk and not be faint. The Lord will grant you sufficient grace to remain steadfast and diligent, maintain high standards of excellence, and live each day with dignity and integrity.

God has good plans for you (Jeremiah 29:11). Dedicate yourself to a bigger course larger than yourself. Discover the power within you and embark on serving humanity through your God-given gifts.

Making a Difference and Soaring

I started my career as a humble bank clerk at Barclays Bank of Kenya. From the lessons of my parents, I was determined to excel and make a career in banking.

I worked hard and ventured into the foreign exchange area, which many people avoided as it was considered challenging at the time. This would open an opportunity to venture into Human Resources - People management and development.

While on a Foreign Exchange and Trade Finance staff training in Karen, Nairobi, a team from the UK global headquarters was visiting. They happened to come into the training room where I was making a presentation from a group activity. They were impressed with my understanding of the subject matter and my presentation delivery skills. They thought I was a trainer, only to be informed that I was a participant. They advised the then Head of Training, late Mrs. Janice Mwosa (may her soul rest in eternity peace), "You should get her onto the training team."

I showed up in the trainers' interviews the following week, and I recall Mrs. Mwosa posing the question, *"Where do you see yourself in three to five years?"*

Without hesitation, I said that I saw myself as Head of Training! Effectively taking over her job! I was successful in the interview and joined the Barclays Staff Training Centre in Karen Nairobi as a Trainer at age twenty-six. My branch manager at the time reckoned that I was too young to be promoted!

I started on an exciting note. I loved training and received consistently positive feedback from participants. Unfortunately, this did not sit well with some of my colleagues. I remember Janice encouraging me in her office. Her words remain with me to this day. She said, *"Joyce, whenever you find yourself facing such antagonism, especially when good reports are received from those who matter, know that you have something more and bigger than your critics."* Three years later, Mrs Mwosa retired, and I was appointed Head of Training!

I moved on to serve in the East and Southern Africa region. While this was an exciting and fulfilling new regional assignment, it was not without its share of challenges. As my star continued to shine, the obstacles increased. I had a boss who believed in hurting others in order to feel powerful. She made my work life unbearable, but I never gave up. I remained diligent and maintained high standards of performance.

When the dream is huge and beyond you the odds don't matter. Always keep your eyes on the goal and go for it. God makes everything beautiful at His time.

I advanced to serve in the international arena. I continue to make a difference in peoples' lives, helping them be the best they can be for the glory of God.

At God's time, when your cup overflows with joy, happiness, peace of mind, remember to pour some of it into someone else's cup. Share these blessings with joy. It's more blessed to give than to receive. Give with a good heart expecting nothing in return.

Transcending: Blessed Beyond Borders

A renewed mindset. Expanded territory.

God answers prayers. He knows our needs even before we ask. His Word encourages us to ASK - Ask, Seek, and Knock. Ask and it shall be given to you; Seek and you shall find; Knock and the door shall be opened for you. Do not shy from praying BOLD prayers.

The Bold Prayer of Jabez. 1 Chronicles 4:10

"Jabez cried out to the God of Israel saying, "Oh, that you would bless me and enlarge my territory! Let your hand be with me and keep me from harm so that I will be free from pain". And God granted his request.

God is gracious to us. He grants us His favour according to His riches in glory. He is able to do exceedingly, abundantly, beyond all that we might ask or think.

New Horizons. Stepping out of my comfort zone, embracing change, doing something different, being somewhere different. I claim and hold onto my blessings wherever I step with my feet. I seek new horizons and embrace fresh abundance as a beacon of hope and change in new places.

I relocated to Lusaka, Zambia, from my beloved homeland, Nairobi, Kenya, with my two children. Ryan had just become a teen, and Ian was a toddler at about three years old. Following the loss of their loving father and my dearest friend Mike, I was overwhelmed with grief. I had taken some time off for vacation from a senior role in the bank to reflect on the next steps.

God works in unique ways. In the afternoon, before our departure to our holiday destination, I received a call from a regional organisation. They had sight of my resume and asked if I would be interested in a Human Resources Expert role for a regional project that was being funded by the European Union. I confirmed that I would be interested and requested that they send me more information via email.

Upon arrival at our hotel in Dubai with my children, I went to the business centre to check if the email was in my inbox. I was pleasantly surprised to read an email from the regional organisation inviting me for an interview and confirming that my travel and accommodation would be fully funded! I travelled to Lusaka, Zambia after our holiday for the interview. A couple of weeks later, I received the good news that I was successful in the interviews.

I took a bold step and left my comfort zone and relocated to a new country with my two children, Ryan, and Ian. I had to let go and let God. My children are my priority. Adapting to a new place, church, culture, food, school, friends, and work culture in a regional organisation, was challenging. However, I was determined to excel. I drew strength from the words of Deuteronomy 8:7-9, *"For the LORD your God is bringing you into a good land - a land with streams and pools of water, with springs flowing in the valleys and hills; a land where bread will not be scarce and you will lack nothing; a land where the rocks are iron and you can dig copper out of the hills."* Zambia is among the top ten copper producing countries. This was a confirmation that God was directing my steps. The transition went well, and Ryan successfully graduated from High school at Lusaka International Community School (LICS) to join the Queensland University of Technology in Brisbane, Australia. Ian blossomed at LICS and was awarded Top Primary School Instrumentalist at the LICS Arts Academy. My star was also shining at work. I was at my happy place.

However, a valley moment happened. The work environment became toxic, Finances were low, COVID happened, and I still had to pay University fees for Ryan. It was a long, dry season. I had one resolve: I had to go through the storm. I would not risk stopping in the middle of the storm for the sake of my children. I thank God that my little sister Nancy came through in my hour of need supporting and encouraging Ryan. A circle of dear friends also stepped in to help. At God's perfect time, He heard my cry and opened a door that moved me from the valley to the mountaintop. I had to take another audacious step and relocate to the United Kingdom to start a new appointment at an International Organisation. In this transition, I was encouraged by the words in Deuteronomy 31:8 *"The LORD himself goes before you, Joyce, and will be with you; He will never leave you nor forsake you. Do not be afraid; do not be discouraged."*

It has been a rewarding adventure. Ryan is a graduate mechatronic engineer in Brisbane, Australia; Ian is thriving at St Edmund's College, UK; and I'm having a rewarding career in London while also serving the community at Hertford St Andrews Church, UK. God has been gracious to us. He is able to turn mourning into dancing, give beauty for ashes, and restore what the locusts have eaten.

Gratitude Anthem. *"Give thanks to the LORD, call on His name, make known among the nations what He has done. Sing to Him, sing praise to Him; tell of all His wonderful acts"* Psalm 105:1-2. As we sang in the youth choir - *He has done so much for me, I cannot tell it all.* Indeed, I'm overwhelmed by the goodness of God.

In memory of my mother, her favorite song resonates very well with this wisdom.

Count your blessings, name them one by one;

Count your blessings, see what God has done;

Count your blessings, name them one by one;

And it will surprise you, what the Lord has done.

Fulfillment. I'm grateful for the servant leadership demonstrated and passed on to me by my parents. They served humanity with a clean heart, expecting nothing in return. I'm conscious that as I transcend to greatness, I'm representing them for giving their all and moulding us to be the best we could ever be. This is unmerited favour. I will always value and exemplify humility in greatness.

A mother's echo. *"Rejoice in the Lord always, I will say it again Rejoice! Let your gentleness be evident to all. The LORD is near."* Philippians 4:4-5. I can hear my mother's voice as she repeated these words. They are a constant reminder to remain steadfast in Faith.

In His generosity, the almighty God catapulted me from Molo in Kenya via Lusaka, Zambia, to an iconic address at the renowned Pall Mall in London, United Kingdom! He is an awesome God. He makes everything beautiful in His time. He did it for me, He can do it for you.

I'm blessed beyond measure; my cup overflows with joy, peace, and praise, from a little girl in the Molo highlands in Kenya to the iconic city of London, United Kingdom. Indeed,

*"No eye has seen, no ear has heard, no mind has conceived what God has prepared for those who love Him."*1 Corinthians 2:9.

Surely goodness and love will follow me all the days of my life, and I will dwell in the house of the LORD forever.

Amen.

ABOUT AUTHOR
Joyce Kamau

Joyce was born and brought up in the Kenyan Highlands in Molo. She is a loving mother of two awesome boys, a young Graduate Mechatronic Engineer, and a vibrant Teen.

She is an International Human Resource Business Partner, a #1 International Best-Selling Author, Certified Leadership and Mind Coach, a member of the International Coaching Community (UK), The Creators Club (Lambent Coaching UK), a resourceful, ideas and supportive community that is focused on creatively defeating VUCA - Volatility, Uncertainty, Complexity, and Ambiguity.

Joyce has been personally mentored by Joseph O'Connor, Author of Coaching the Brain and the founder of the Neuroscience Coaching Centre, UK and The Creators Club; Renowned Results Coach, Jon Talarico under the transformational Thinking Into Results (TIR) coaching programme, and the world's most renowned motivational speaker Les Brown as his prodigy.

A Mind Coach student of Unestahl Mental Training (UMT) of Sweden, Ms Kamau is enthusiastic about helping individuals unlock their full potential and be the best they can be.

A Co-founder of SOAR Coaching Solutions Limited, Joyce lives in the United Kingdom and is dedicated to providing purposeful solutions through a journey of self-awareness and self-discovery.

Connect with Joyce:

magiri@soarcoachingsolutions.com

info@soarcoachingsolutions.com

THERE WAS FEAR NO MORE
By Carmen Cadena

Fear thou not; for I am with thee: be not dismayed; for I am thy God: I will strengthen thee; yea, I will help thee; yea, I will uphold thee with the right hand of my righteousness.

Isaiah 41:10

FEAR. Such a common thing to live our lives by, many times without even having the awareness that most of our choices are influenced by fear or most of us make choices based on fear. Every choice I've made for as long as I can remember was influenced by fear. The fear of dying and facing the abyss of the unknown. Fear of pain, a specter that loomed at every turn. Fear of loss and the pain of emptiness it will leave behind and the fear of rejection. No fear seemed foreign to me, for each found a place within my heart –or at least, that is what it felt like, and righteously so.

My past left its marks on the canvas of my life; you can read more about my story in *The Greatness in You* and *Get Up! God Is Not Done with You Yet!* Two anthologies that bear witness to the journey that forged my path. Early hardships shaped the very essence of my being. The jarring experiences I was exposed to at an early age took control of my life and my logic. Instead of learning the skills to blossom as a normal little girl, I learned to navigate the world through the lens of survival.

Feelings of restlessness and stress became normal to me. I often sought after the threat even if there was no threat at all. I became so keen to notice all the things that could go wrong before I considered all the things that could go right. A constant fight-or-flight physical state flooded my veins with adrenaline and cortisol -always ready to fight, other times ready to run. Our brain, by default, is programmed to fight or flight in the presence of danger, but what happens when a person is often exposed to much uncertainty, and there is no proper structure within the home that allows your fight-or-flight response mechanism to settle back to its normal state? Then what our brain does is remain on that high level of fear. Unfortunately, for those of us raised amidst the harsh embrace of poverty, violence, and relentless uncertainty — fear becomes our companion. We learn to distrust, lie, and manipulate in order to feel some sense of control. Unfortunately, I did not have a solid foundation of safety at home since I perceived my grandparents as frail and it worried me that someone would hurt them.

My grandmother's intention was to mold me into a fearless and resilient individual, instilling in me the valor to confront danger. Yet, my deepest yearning was for a carefree childhood, free from the need to suppress my tears. I craved guidance in understanding my emotions, but my grandmother's teachings were limited to what she knew best: fortitude. Despite her efforts to nurture a valiant spirit within me, an undercurrent of profound fear began to influence my decision-making in life. Countless individuals navigate their life paths while swayed by the currents of fear.

One thing I realized in my own journey is the intricate dance between bravery and fear when choices loom before us. It requires profound courage to confront decisions that invoke fear, doesn't it? But does that mean we are devoid of fear altogether? I invite you to reflect on those pivotal moments when you wanted to say "no" but proceeded with a hesitant "yes," or vice versa, driven by the specter of fear. In those instances, did you not also exhibit elements of bravery? Perhaps it was the choice to walk away from a relationship that had ceased to nourish your soul, yet you stayed out of fear. I understand very well what it is like to live in fear, and paradoxically, as we endeavor to evade our fears, we can inadvertently find ourselves ensnared in our fears just like it was jail and addiction for me.

The word of God calls us to be women and men of faith. Yet, how is it that even then, many of us believers still struggle with fear? I understand, as a non-believer, how easy it can sometimes be to live in fear. I say this because I once was a non-believer. But the Bible says:

> *For God hath not given us the spirit of fear; but of power, and of love, and of a sound mind.*

> *2 Timothy 1:17*

Even after my salvation and commitment to follow Christ, I found myself continually plagued by fear. It was through my personal journey that I came to realize this persistence was rooted in our paradigms. Are you familiar with what these paradigms entail? Essentially, our lives are governed by a set of paradigms that have molded the very essence of our being up to this point. They serve as the bedrock upon which our decision-making abilities are founded. In simple terms, our paradigm consists of an intricate web of habits that influence our thought processes, shaped by our past experiences.

Allow me to illustrate this concept with a personal example: *"Well, that's just the way I am. I hate asparagus!"* While that statement might accurately reflect your current feelings, it doesn't imply that you can never develop a liking for asparagus. Given the opportunity to try it multiple times, prepared and cooked in various ways, you can forge new neural pathways in your brain that make the prospect of enjoying asparagus a distinct possibility.

Certainly, for a new neural pathway to form, the new behavior must be practiced repeatedly. Some suggest it takes about 21 times, hence the well-known *"Do this for 21 days or your money back"* adages. However, another research indicates that it may take longer. Whether it's 21 days, a month, a year, or more, one fact remains constant: building a robust neural pathway requires consistent practice of the new habit or behavior. How many repetitions are required? As many as it takes until you've mastered it.

As you continue to read this chapter, I will share with you some tools that I have personally used to break through some of those habits that caused me to be a fearful adult. And I pray that the same tools are a blessing to you and help you in your journey.

In 2013, I made the pivotal decision to finally quit smoking cigarettes, a choice that had long been overdue. Many wondered about the challenges I faced: Was it difficult? Did I experience relapses? How long did it take for me to quit? These were the questions from those contemplating the thought of quitting. My response was candid: "Yes, it was undeniably difficult. Yes, I relapsed. And it took me quite some time."

The difficulty didn't solely stem from the very real withdrawal symptoms of nicotine but also from the constant fixation on the difficulty itself. Paradoxically, the more I dwelled on the hardships of quitting, the more daunting it became. This mental preoccupation inadvertently drew me back towards smoking, resulting in a relapse.

This pattern persisted as I repeatedly attempted to quit, only to find myself falling back into the same old habit without success. So, what gave me the breakthrough to give up smoking once and for all? It was a new habit I was creating, which I will share with you at the end of this chapter, combined with a skill I had learned a while back from one of the many counselors who helped me achieve sobriety. *"You've got to replay the negative tape of all the harm it's caused you. Pair it with an ugly feeling and replay the tape over and over."* Of course, at that point, I did not understand the depth of the message. All I knew was that I did as I was told. I followed directions, and I got sober. Therefore, I knew that if that exercise had worked back then, then it would work to help me quit nicotine. And guess what? It did.

I repeatedly reminded myself of the reason why I did not like smoking anymore, even if part of me still liked it. I utterly repeated to myself: *"I don't like the way I smell. I don't like feeling out of breath. I don't like my raspy voice. I hate to have to ask my daughter to go away so that she doesn't see me smoking."* And without knowing anything about how habits work, I was doing exactly that: changing the programing in my brain. And that is exactly how habits are broken. But remember, a paradigm is a *multitude* of habits, not a single habit. To change a paradigm, you must repeat the new behavior countless times until new programming occurs. One habit at a time!

When can you recognize the establishment of a new habit? It becomes evident when the new way of behaving feels natural, and the old behavior becomes obsolete. Why is this knowledge important? It ties back to the earlier discussion in this chapter when I described my upbringing, emphasizing how I was raised to be brave. This upbringing kept me in a perpetual state of fight or flight, making it more comfortable for me to reside in fear rather than embracing bravery or confronting conflict. And in order for me to bust through the fear, I had to adopt a new way of thinking.

For me, and likely for many others, our upbringing can shape a paradigm rooted in fear. When this occurs, we find ourselves living a life of survival, perpetually watchful our surroundings. We exist in a continuous state of tension ready to fight anything or anyone. We approach life with a cautious eye, ever vigilant to avoid danger. Ironically, the very things we attempt to flee from often become the very forces that chase us and ensnare us.

I never wanted to go to jail. I was scared at the thought of becoming dependent on any substance. Yet, there I was, being transported to the detention center by a Sheriff's bus, where offenders are transported to and from court after being detained for a violation of the law. But God works in mysterious ways, and it was right at that moment that I decided that the path I was on was not the path where I belonged.

Often, we unknowingly attract the troubles we encounter, driven by subconscious forces. Deep within our souls, we all harbor the fundamental desire to feel secure and cherished — an innate need for unconditional love, irrespective of our imperfections. We yearn for those who can see past our flaws and recognize the incredible potential within us, even if it takes time to materialize.

Unfortunately, when we ourselves are not whole and healed, we tend to gravitate towards individuals who share our fears and brokenness. We enter into romantic relationships with others who are similarly yearning. We may not be fully healed or complete, but we offer the comfort of safety and love, receiving it in return. Yet, when these feelings of security and love are threatened, we often return to what is familiar to us: the primal response of fight or flight.

In society, it's common to assign labels when individuals seek therapy. *"She's bipolar," "he's depressed," "she suffers from anxiety."* While these clinical labels are accurate, I believe that for many of us, the root of these afflictions lies in the absence of love and security during critical periods in our lives — particularly during our childhood when we needed nurturing superhero-like parents. At the core of our existence, we all crave acceptance and love, even those who may initially appear seemingly unlovable.

So, what has changed in my life, and how can I teach you what this chapter is about? The title *There Was Fear No More* really occurred to me a few weeks before the chapter was due, and I had to send it to the editor. It happened after a conversation I had had with a few friends on two separate occasions. One conversation happened when a friend of mine said that she was tired of feeling like she needed to ask for permission every time it was time for her to make a choice in her life. Right at that moment, I realized that I, too, sought after someone's permission as if I were afraid to make a decision on my own. But the question remained: why? Why was I waiting for someone else's approval?

The second time occurred when a colleague said to me: *"What is the worst that can happen?"* and encouraged me to dive deeper into that question and play the worst-case scenario in my mind. There I was once again, doing an exercise using my imagination and giving my brain the opportunity to live an experience without actually having to live it, at least not at that time. And then, BOOM! As if by magic, I finally realized that I was living by fear and that it was time to break that paradigm and once and for all practice faith over fear.

There is a Bible verse, in fact, the very first verse I memorized, and I encourage you to do the same. It says:

[5] Trust in the LORD with all thine heart; and lean not unto thine own understanding.
[6] In all thy ways acknowledge him, and he shall direct thy paths

Proverbs 3: 5-6

So, this verse explicitly commands us to what? To trust!

In Who? In the One and Only God.

How? With all our heart. And then it also commands us to lean not unto our own understanding, meaning don't try to make sense of things on your own. God's wisdom is far beyond our own, and let's remember that many times our prayers are answered with a "No" because God has a greater "*Yes*" coming our way. But it also says in ALL [our] ways; what does ALL mean? All means ALL. Not halfway, not sometimes, not with this and not with that, and we acknowledge Him by asking for wisdom every step of the way. Not only in some ways. And this is where this verse gets really great. The promise. Of what? He shall direct OUR paths, which brings me to my next point of the chapter.

WHAT IS THE TOOL TO OVERCOME FEAR?

PRAYER.

BECAUSE PRAYER WILL, IN EXCHANGE, REPLACE FEAR WITH FAITH.

What is prayer? Making time for God, just how you look forward to speaking to a friend. Jesus is YOUR friend and has found favor in you. The fact that you are here reading this chapter was meant to happen right now. It is perhaps an answered prayer. I know that I am here today because of my mom's prayers. She gave her life to Jesus the minute that she saw me lost in my addiction. Prayer is a weapon of bravery. It is surrendering what you think you know, and talking to God like you would with a friend. It is being vulnerable. It is hoping. There is not a prayer that you need to memorize. There are no hand signs that the Bible talks about that you need to know. Some of my prayers sound like I am talking to my mother, other times like I am speaking to my pastor, and others like I am speaking to my best friend. I have even said, *"Um, Jesus, are you not listening right now?? I need the answer to be crystal clear; make it so that I KNOW it is coming from you. Slap me in the face with your answer, please. Thank you!"*

Which brings me to my next and final point:

How do I pray?

I pray from the heart. Even in moments of confusion when I can't comprehend the reasons behind certain events, I remain thankful. I am grateful for the ability to see, feel, and breathe, and for the love I have experienced—even when my heart may be broken at the time of prayer. There is an abundance of reasons to be grateful for, and one doesn't need to possess all the answers to open their heart in surrender.

How has prayer helped me?

As I shared earlier, after I got saved, the new habit I was creating was using prayer in my journey to quit smoking cigarettes. It was the first tool I used to quit smoking cigarettes. I suddenly got the strength to replay the tape in my head of how distasteful it was to smoke. Prayer gave me the strength not to give up.

How can prayer help you?

Well, look at your life right now and write a rigorous, honest, and moral inventory of yourself. How are you doing? What is hurting you? What is not working for you? Who hurt you? How's letting go of that resentment that set you off a while back? Who do you need to forgive? What keeps you awake at night? Why are you so afraid? I am sure you can think of more questions, but if you're able to, please write them down and answer those questions. Really, answer them!

Make time alone and write it all down. Cry it out. Let it out. Let go and let God.

How to make prayer THE number one weapon in your life.

You start by praying as often as you can. As much as you can. For as long as you can. For anyone you can. And even just to check-in. "Thank you, Jesus, I feel fine today." And you memorize scripture because "out of the depths of the heart the mouth speaketh." Mat (12:34)

Thy word have I hid in my heart that I might not sin against thee
(Psalm 119:11)

My prayer for you is that you accept Jesus in your heart and that you build a solid relationship with Him. He is the foundation of my life, and this chapter was too short to really share all the stuff that happened to me, but just know that if Jesus was able to transform someone like me and use me into a vessel to spread His love and word, he could do it for anyone. I should've been dead many times, but I am not, and I feel that that is the power of prayer. He has transformed my life, and I am not sinless, but as a Christian, I definitely sin less and that is ALL thanks to Him and all glory and Honor to His name.

ABOUT AUTHOR
Carmen Cadena

Carmen was born and raised by her grandmother in Mexico. At the age of fifteen, her visit to the United States turned into an unforeseen permanent transition, propelling her into a world of adaptation and transformation.

In the midst of not speaking English and trying to fit into a whole new culture, Carmen found comfort and strength in something she had loved since she was a kid: writing. When she moved to the United States with her mom, she kept the connection strong with her loved ones in Mexico by writing heartfelt letters. It was like a lifeline, bridging the gap between her new life and her family and friends, she left behind who did not have a landline to talk on.

Determined to forge her own path, Carmen overcame hurdles, completing high school. Driven by her thirst for knowledge and a profound fascination with the human mind and society, she pursued an associate degree in Social and Behavioral Science. This academic pursuit deepened her understanding of the intricate workings of the mind, the profound influence of society on individual choices, and the limitless potential for personal growth.

Although Carmen's personal life bore the weight of profound challenges—battles with anxiety, depression, and substance abuse—she emerged as a survivor, transcending the scars of her traumatic experiences. Today, she not only thrives but devotes herself to empowering others through the transformative power of writing.

Carmen's indomitable spirit propelled her to become a best-selling author, combining her love for writing and healing. She exemplifies the unwavering power of the human spirit to triumph over adversity. Her life's story serves as an inspiration, reminding us that with unwavering perseverance and the transformative power of writing, we can overcome even the most challenging circumstances that life presents.

Connect with Carmen

IG: @coachcarmencadena

FB: www.facebook.com/becauseyourstorymatters

Email: carmenspeakstoday@gmail.com

S.O. ❦ C.A.N. ❦ Y.O.U.
By Dr. Sonya Howell Barrow

"I can do all things through Christ who strengthens me." NKJV
Philippians 4:13

"A winner is a dreamer who never gives up." ~ Nelson Mandela

A S I embark on the next chapter in my life, I am reminded that time is of the essence, and it will not wait for me. Because this is my life and my story, I realize that it is imperative for me to always *"show up"* for myself and love myself from the very beginning. Since I own the pen and paper of my story, I will narrate my life's story the way that I want it to be told.

Though I refuse to allow undesirable thoughts to control my actions and behaviors, oftentimes, my mind is clouded with unanswered questions. Sometimes, I wonder if decisions that were made for me, to me, or by me thus far have been the best decisions for me. But then, I am reminded of my belief in God and the importance of trusting the process. So, with that in mind, I remain focused on my future and my desire to unleash my fullest potential.

VICTORIOUS TRANSFORMATION

Over the years, I have evolved into a woman embodied with the strength and serenity to accept those things in my life that are not easily changeable. However, with wisdom and courage, I am able to eliminate things that are changeable. Simply because I know that with God, anything is possible; therefore, in my quest for success, I will **be fearless** as I embrace my self-worth and self-love because I will accept nothing less. I will **be inspired** as I take chances on those who are ready and willing to take chances on me. I will **be resilient** as I defy individuals and situations that do not appreciate me and the great qualities that I have to offer. I will **be empowered** as I remain mentally focused on the beautifully, empowered, triumphant (B.E.T.) me.

As I continue to evolve into your next best you, I will pursue my passions with love and unwavering purpose. I will never discredit myself or quit on myself. Instead, I will excitedly cheer for my number one fan, me. If I can do something good, I can do something better than I have ever imagined. Positive results matter to me because I know that the best things come to those who wait.

So, whenever I look at my smiling reflection in the mirror, I gather my strength, determination, and confidence, then repeat to myself, if the next person can accomplish their dreams, goals, and ambitions, *S.O. ❦ C.A.N. ❦ Y.O.U.*

S – SACRIFICES: Throughout my life, I have made decisions that were uncomfortable but necessary. Simply because many things in life are never easily attainable, in the past, I have made many mental, physical, emotional, and financial sacrifices today as I prepared for a better tomorrow. Fortunately, my maturity, self-discipline, and self-control enhanced my ability to make personal sacrifices that were in my best interest. **I make sacrifices.**

O – OBEDIENCE: I did not always understand the importance of obedience to my mother, grandmother, and God. However, now that I am much older, I have a better understanding of obedience and my purpose. Life is my school, and experiences are my teachers. With obedience, I realize that God would not have chosen to give me life or provide me with the gifts of knowledge and common sense for this life if he did not think that I was worthy and capable. I know that I am a work in progress, and I still require God's continuous oversight and training to help me stride confidently through my life with purpose and passion. **I have obedience.**

C – COURAGE: Though I always attempt to maintain an unwavering stance during moments of uncertainty, sometimes I must embrace my animal instinct. Other times, I continuously recite one of my daily affirmations, "Nothing beats a failure but a try." I am reminded of yesteryear when my beloved grandmother Mary and beloved Aunt Flo recited this affirmation to me during my times of uncertainty. This affirmation is powerful because it stimulates my courage. Then, I am confidently able to keep going. I realize that for me to finish, I must start. **I have courage.**

A – ATTITUDE OF GRATITUDE: I thank God for HIS mercy, grace, and the many blessings bestowed upon my life. I appreciate those times when situations did not work out in my favor. Many times, I was unaware of situations that I had been protected from. However, because I have an attitude of gratitude, I am forever grateful for the protection and avoidance of situations and troubles along my path. More importantly, with protection, I was able to navigate through the midst of chaos and confusion as I prepared for something better. **I have an attitude of gratitude.**

N – NEVER QUIT ATTITUDE: No one is perfect. I refuse to allow negative thoughts such as fear, doubt, weakness, or unworthiness to define my life's choices. Instead, I recite positive affirmations to myself daily to ensure that I remain mindful of my strengths, weaknesses, capabilities, and potential. My never quit attitude is empowering because it is my internal defensive mechanism. Besides, quitting will never be an option for me because I refuse to self-sabotage the greatness God has in store for me. So, I am not afraid to take positive risks that are in my best interest to ensure that I level up to the greatness destined for me. This is my life, and I will tell the greatness of my story the way that I want it to be told. **I have a never quit attitude.**

Y – YES: I strive to maintain a positive mindset that allows me to manifest favorable outcomes for my future goals, dreams, and ambitions because, "yes," anything is possible. Also, I am reminded that if God can bring me to it, HE will bring me through it. So, I avoid naysayers, distractions, and anything else that is not in alignment with my purpose and the plans that God has for me and my life. **I say yes.**

O – ON TIME: As I embark on my dreams, goals, and ambitions, it is imperative for me to show up for myself on time. With self-love, I am able to appreciate all of my personal qualities, good, bad, and ugly. I know my worth and what I have to offer. Ultimately, I will ignite my ꙮ FIRE without hesitation as I strive to turn my dreams into reality with God's timing. **I am on time.**

U – UNSTOPPABLE: I refuse to allow negative thoughts to control my actions. Instead, I recite positive affirmations that guide my thoughts so that I remain focused on what's most important: me. I am unstoppable because "I can." My mental superpower is that I do not allow words such as "no, can't or cannot" to define me. Instead, I encourage myself with positive words such as, *"Yes, can, of course, and absolutely."* As I look forward to my future endeavors, I will always be reminded of my previous achievements. Ultimately, I have surpassed your next best you because I am the next best you. **I am unstoppable.**

This is your life and your destiny. Though our lives are filled with endless possibilities, self-love is critical for our mental and emotional well-being. Now is the time for you to take total control of your life. As life continues to knock at the door, will you deny yourselves opportunities? Or will you accept challenges? Do not worry about impressing individuals if their opinions of you are irrelevant. As you walk into the proverbial unfamiliar room of opportunities, smile, hold your head up high, and gracefully walk into the room as if you own it. Do not allow others to intimidate you. You deserve to be in the room, too. Some goals may take longer than others, but all goals are attainable. Remember, you are not a failure. You have simply not succeeded yet. If you should stumble and fall, simply pick yourself up, dust yourself off, and keep going. Nothing beats a failure but a try. So, show up for yourself and try harder.

You are not a finished product; you are a work in progress. Therefore, your today's and your tomorrows should be filled with your roadmap to success. More importantly, if you do not take the time to invest in yourself today, then who will take the time to invest in you tomorrow? So, continue to *nourish* your self-love, *elevate* your mental health, *exceed* your personal goals, and **transcend** into *"Your Next Best You."* You know your worth, and you have a lot to offer. Promise yourself that you will live up to your fullest potential, stop looking for yourself in the wrong places, ignite your internal 🔥 FIRE, and find yourself. **Be fearless** and take the chance on you. **Be inspired** to take on new adventures that will encourage you. **Be resilient** and refuse to allow negative obstacles to obstruct your path and discourage you. **Be empowered** to level up to the dreams and goals for you. Be confident. You are a winner! Whenever you look at your reflection in the mirror, never forget that if the next person can do it, **S.O.** 🔥 **C.A.N.** 🔥 **Y.O.U.**

🔥 FIRE "Igniting The Joy and Love Within."

🔥 *Be Fearless.*
🔥 *Be Inspired.*
🔥 *Be Resilient.*
🔥 *Be Empowered.*

With Love,

Sonya

ABOUT AUTHOR
Dr. Sonya Howell Barrow

Sonya LaVonka Howell Barrow is an Authorpreneur, Life Coach, CEO of The SoJaDe Group, LLC and founder of Authorpreneur Sonya. She was born at Fort Gordon, Georgia and raised between Augusta and Warrenton, Georgia.

She is a mother of two and United States Army Chief Warrant Officer Five - (Retired). She earned her Master's Degree in Cyber Security from the University of Maryland, University College. If she isn't spending time with family and friends, she is always trying to motivate others by letting them know that the "glass is always half full, never half empty." She strives to inspire and empower people to live their best lives that are filled with confidence, self-awareness, and personal growth.

Sonya is a co-author of a very inspirational and powerful anthology entitled "More Than A Conqueror Volume 1." Her chapter within the book is "Better Days Are Coming...Joy Comes In The Morning."

She is a featured author of the anthology entitled "The CHAMPION Mindset Volume 1." Her chapter within the book is "The Courage To Evolve."

Sonya is penning several solo book projects. Her first book projects, entitled "Sonya's Little Book Of Quotes: A Coffee Table Guide of FIRE Inspirations" and "Sonya's Little Book Of Quotes: A Coffee Table Guide of FIRE Inspirations: For Journaling," are pending release.

Sonya is also penning her memoir series entitled, "She Is Me! Defying My Life's Obstacles by Not Becoming a Statistic Book-I: The Struggle Is Real," and the second book of her memoir entitled, "She Is Me! Defying My Life's Obstacles by Not Becoming a Statistic Book-II: Smile for Me."

Sonya has also contributed to "Letters of Love & Legacy: Heartfelt Expressions to Those We Love."

Connect with Sonya:

EMAIL: hello@sonyahowellbarrow.com

WEBSITE: http://www.sonyahowellbarrow.com

LINKTREE: https://linktr.ee/sonyahowellbarrow

FACEBOOK:

https://www.facebook.com/authorpreneursonya

INSTAGRAM:

https://www.instagram.com/authorpreneursonya

LINKEDIN:

https://www.linkedin.com/in/sonyahowellbarrow/

LOSING ME FINDING I AM

By Denise Augustus

I've had days when I looked in the mirror, wondering who I am while questioning my worth and value. I've also had days where I stood confident, knowing I am loved, valued, and chosen by God. I want to share with you how I transitioned to the beautiful reality of knowing my Identity is found and rooted in Christ and Him alone, Knowing I can now rest in Him in all my imperfections without doubting His love for me, Understanding that He molds and shapes me into everything he calls me to be, And most importantly, knowing that if He's done it for me, He can do it for you too!

Before giving my life to the Lord, I was entirely in the dark. I didn't know who I was or why I was created. You see, I grew up in the foster care system and bounced from home to home from about 6, with very little control over what I would eat, where I would sleep, or who I would call my family. From a very early age, I remember my biological mother calling me the ugly duckling because I was darker than my siblings. Why couldn't I have turned out like them, I thought. After seeing that even in foster care, they took precedence over me, I believed all the more the ugly duckling was who I was and unknowingly attached it to my identity.

Being that I believed the negative thoughts and lies spoken over me, I began to live my life like they were true, so it became my reality. I didn't know who I was, so I allowed others to tell me who I was or become what they needed me to be. Little did I know my true Identity would be revealed to me in a way I would have never suspected.

At 14 years old, I accepted Jesus as my Lord and Savior. It was like nothing I ever felt or experienced before. After hanging out with the wrong person and smoking marijuana for the first time, it was laced with PCP (also known as "Angel Dust"). It landed me in the hospital, crying to the Lord for my life. This was the consequence of my desperate wanting to be accepted. I was now desperate to know if the God I was crying out to was real and would somehow save me from the horror I was experiencing. The fear of death gripped me, and I knew If God didn't show up, I wouldn't make it.

After repeatedly crying out to the Lord, He came to me in a vision and showed me how much He loved me and was always with me. The Lord also revealed that I was not an accident, and He had a purpose and a plan for my life. Not only did he save me, but He completely healed my mind and body from what could have been a fatal outcome. And most importantly, He gave me Identity!

Although I had a new Identity, I realized It was only head knowledge. I had no understanding of who I was in Christ. I didn't know how to live in the reality of my new Identity or utilize the tools God had given me to live from a place of victory. Although what the Lord did for me forever lived in my heart, and there was no denying His existence or power, I soon struggled with my walk with Him. I was back to allowing the lies of the enemy and the cares of life to weigh me down.

As time passed, I doubted if I was truly valuable to God. With no actual understanding of how to grow in Christ, I found myself striving for what God has already provided for me. I eventually married and had a beautiful daughter in my early 20s. I soon began to struggle in my marriage. I became upset with God and found myself at times doubting the plans He had for me. I would go back and forth between wanting to serve God and seeking fulfillment outside Him. I was double-minded and not anchored in the truth of God's word.

I was in my 30s, still in the habit of people-pleasing and seeking validation from others. Never did I feel good enough or accepted. The constant comparing myself with others led me deeper into insecurities and depression. I was scared to socialize and speak my mind out of fear of sounding dumb and believing I was a nobody. Even around other believers, I felt inferior. Knowing that I was still struggling with my Identity after all these years of being saved left me feeling discouraged and defeated. Why wasn't I joyful and walking in victory like everyone else? What's wrong with me? I thought.

All my questions left me feeling Angry, depressed, and frustrated. I also allowed the opinions and actions of others to affect me and control how I viewed myself. Somehow, I thought by coming to the Lord, my insecurities, Anger, and feelings of worthlessness would somehow disappear. Shamefully, I was disappointed in God. My life seemed to be moving in a constant up-and-down cycle that I couldn't break free from. Despite all of it, I knew my life was purposeless without God. I was tired and mentally and spiritually at rock bottom. And to my surprise, that's exactly where I needed to be to come to the beautiful place of surrender. To come to the place that left me no choice but to lose myself so I could find I AM.

Have you ever felt like you were in a similar cycle? Maybe you've been born-again for a long time, but if you're honest, you realize you don't know the Lord as you should. Perhaps you feel distant from Him, and it's embarrassing to admit where you're at spiritually. Trust me; I get it because that's precisely where I was when I finally surrendered and let God do what only He could.

Although I've been saved for many years, the problem was I spent so much of my time striving, meaning I was trying to do everything in my own strength and ability, trying to look the part of someone full of Joy and walking in complete victory. But I had no Joy or peace inside me, and most of the time, I lived in condemnation, constantly replaying all my mistakes and failures in my mind while attaching them to my Identity. I was trying to clean myself up instead of letting God clean me up and finish the work He had already started In me. When God began to open my eyes to this, I finally realized why, in Philippians 1:6, The Apostle Paul says, God, who began the good work within you, will continue His work until it is finally finished on the day Christ Jesus returns.

In Matthew 11:28, Jesus said Come to me, all you who are weary and burdened, and I will give you rest. Take my yoke upon you and learn from me, for I am gentle and humble in heart, and you will find rest for your souls. For my yoke is easy, and my burden is light. I didn't fully understand this until I was tired. Tired of pretending, Tired of meeting other people's expectations, Tired of not seeing all that God had in store for me, tired of being timid and living in fear of what man thinks about me, Tired of trying to find fulfillment in the world when I knew it could only be found in the one trustworthy source which is Christ Jesus, And most importantly tired of giving the enemy control of my mind and being driven by my emotions. I was burdened and tired of carrying the weight of it all. I wanted to exchange all that I had for all that God had for me. No longer did I want to be victorious in appearance, but I desperately wanted true victory on the inside of me.

Through a deep desire to be free and crying out to God, The Lord began to show me that I had a heart problem. He didn't mean the organ in our body that pumps blood, but in the word of God, the heart refers to our mind, will, and emotions. It's the spiritual side of us and the place where our feelings and desires begin. I learned that the enemy loves to attack our minds. It's the main area where the enemy attacks. Our thoughts trigger our emotions, which then influence our actions. A saying goes: Our life goes in the direction of our strong thoughts. And let me tell you, it's true, and the word of God confirms this repeatedly. Once I discovered this, I started searching for how to overcome the battle with my mind and emotions that has kept me bound for so long. I found that it all started with a deep desire to change. Not only did I search the scriptures, but I Sought out mentorship, prayer, and accountability partners. God also began to reveal to me through books like Joyce Meyers's Battlefield of the Mind and Craig Groeschel's Winning The War In Your Mind how I was opening the door to the enemy for attacks and how to close the door to guard my heart. In Proverbs 4:23-7 it says, Above all else, guard your heart, for everything you do flows from it. Everything I was experiencing, from the feelings of unworthiness, low self-esteem, timidity, and looking to the world for fulfillment, all stemmed from seeds planted in my mind in the form of thoughts.

I allowed these thoughts to take up residence in my mind instead of immediately kicking them out or seeing if they lined up with the word of God. In the same way, it was a decision for me to believe the negative thoughts planted in my mind; it's also a decision for me to accept the truth of God's word. If I accepted the fact, I would have warm feelings to confirm that truth. I realized just like salvation is not a matter of feelings but declaration, so is Identity! It says in Romans 10:9-11 that if you confess with your mouth the Lord Jesus and believe in your heart that God has raised Him from the dead, you will be saved for it is with your heart that you believe and are justified, and it is with your mouth that you confess and are saved. Notice that confession and Believing with your heart go hand in hand. We discussed how your heart consists of your mind, will, and emotions. So, when we accept Christ as Lord, we confess with our mouths and believe with our minds, will, and emotions. The same goes for our identity; we are to confess what the Lord says about us out of our mouths and believe with our minds, will, and emotions. Our mind will lead, and then our feelings will follow. Remember, Identity is not a matter of feelings but declarations! God never intended for us to be ruled by our emotions but for us to have dominion over them. We control our emotions by being intentional about what thoughts we allow to take up residence in our minds and meditating on the word of God while consistently asking the Holy Spirit for help and guidance every step of the way. I'm so glad the Holy Spirit opened my eyes to this powerful truth.

I used to imagine God using me in a mighty way, but at the time, I didn't realize I was using a significant key to unlock all God has for me. You see, God has gifted us with so many beautiful gifts, and imagination is one of them. Through imagination, things are created. Everything we see has all started in the imagination, whether God's imagination or humans'. Napoleon Hill wrote, *"The imagination is the workshop wherein are fashioned all plans created by man."* In Genesis, it talks about how we were created in the image and likeness of God, so we know that God is a creator; therefore, so are we. When I imagined the great things God had in store for me and believed I would see them come to pass, doors would open. For example, after everything the enemy tried to do to get me to doubt who I am in Christ and the plans God had for me, I finally decided to come into alignment with what God said about me. I believed in my heart that one day, I would write a book and, preach the gospel worldwide, and live my life for the Glory of God. Well, guess what? Here I am, writing my first anthology ever!

God is so Faithful! Additionally, I recently became a certified Life Coach and an ordained minister of the Gospel.

All Glory to God!! I once had a word spoken over me years ago that I want to declare, *"What your past disqualifies you for, God is Qualifying you for."* I can stand confident and tell you that today, this prophetic word of the Lord has been fulfilled in my life! I know this only happened because I stood In faith and chose to see things from God's perspective. The Lord's word cannot return unto Him void, so the only thing standing in the way of the promises and plans of God for your life and them coming to pass your belief and imagination.

As Children of God and Kingdom citizens, we are called to imagine all the great things that could happen. There is so much power in our imagination, and throughout the bible, God asks us to use this special gift. Faith and imagination work together, and Hebrews 11 says, Faith is the substance of things hoped for, the evidence of things not seen. Knowing this truth has helped me not only imagine a reality above my current circumstances but believe it will come to pass and see it come to pass. I went from accepting the natural reality of me not having a degree, feeling unaccomplished, feeling unwanted and unloved, and being a prisoner to my negative thoughts and emotions to now seeing myself how God sees me, knowing the Lord is a Father to the fatherless and a mother to the motherless, to believe I can do all things through Christ who strengthens me!!

Here I am now, ordained with a Life Coach Certification and writing my first Anthology with my life experiences as my qualification. What the enemy meant for evil, God turned it around for my good! The part that never ceases to amaze me is knowing the best is yet to come! And if He's done it for me, He will surely do the same for you!

ABOUT AUTHOR
Denise Augustus

Denise Augustus is a Certified Life Coach and Ordained Minister; she studied Youth Ministry with a concentration in Counseling at Nyack College in Nyack, New York, and is a H.S. graduate of Kingston High School in Kingston, N.Y. Denise also studied at the New School of Radio and Television.

Her professional interests focus on being a life coach and fulfilling her calling as an ordained minister. She has experience in missions worldwide, including Uganda, England, Montserrat, and Antigua.

She desires to see people of every background and culture set free and come to the full knowledge and understanding of their God-given identity, teaching them how to live a life of victory and power as God intended for them from the beginning of creation.

She is a leader of women, including her leadership role in women's Ministry at her church, End Times Harvesters International, and a lead host of "Kingdom Identity Podcast." Her passion for ministry is birthed from her greatest passion of all: seeing women from all walks of life and backgrounds live their lives for the glory of God. Her goal is to continue to live out the Great Commission, traveling the world and preaching the gospel.

Connect with Denise

daugustus44@gmail.com

MIRROR TALK
By Karlita Renata Green

WHAT we say about ourselves is a direct reflection of how we see ourselves. Our self-view impacts our thought life, our spiritual life, our relationships and most importantly it affects the purpose we were created for. After overcoming adversity after adversity, the one thing that has been constant on my journey is mirror talk. What I have said to myself in each season of my life has determined how I've reacted to each trial I've been faced with.

Unveiling the Power Within

In the journey of life, we often find ourselves facing trials that leave scars on our hearts and minds. These scars can shape our perceptions of ourselves and our abilities, often leading us down a path of self-doubt and negativity. Despite these shadows of despair, there is hope and healing waiting to be discovered. For those who have faced domestic violence and the heartbreak of divorce, this powerful tool can be a guiding light towards self-discovery and self-love.

Unveiling the Shadows: A Journey of Survival

As a survivor of domestic violence and the aftermath of divorce, you have navigated through treacherous waters, emerging stronger and more resilient than ever before. These experiences, although painful, have carved a path for your self-discovery. They are also what makes us relatable to those of us who have faced these same life-changing events. Through the darkness, you have found the strength within to rebuild your life, and now it's time to embrace a practice that will amplify that strength – Mirror Talk.

Mirror Talk Defined: Conversations with the Soul

Mirror Talk is more than just a series of words spoken to one's reflection; it's a conversation with the deepest parts of your being. Imagine standing before a mirror, locking eyes with the person staring back at you – that person who has triumphed over adversity, who has weathered the storms of life. Mirror Talk invites you to address this person, to acknowledge their strength and courage, and to speak words of kindness and encouragement directly to them. It's also an opportunity to give yourself permission to become the new version of yourself after overcoming adversity.

The Power of Self-Affirmation: Rebuilding from Within

In a world that often bombards us with negative messages, self-affirmation becomes a vital weapon in our arsenal. The power of Mirror Talk lies in its ability to counteract the self-doubt that can linger after surviving trials. By repeating positive affirmations, you are rewriting the narrative of your self-worth. *"I am strong." "I am resilient." "I am deserving of love and happiness."* These words become a shield against the lingering doubts that may try to creep in.

Healing the Scars: Embracing Self-Love

After surviving domestic violence and divorce, it's easy to internalize the blame, to carry the weight of guilt and shame. But the journey towards healing requires shedding these burdens and embracing self-love. Mirror Talk is a practice of self-compassion, a way to nurture the wounded parts of ourselves with the balm of encouraging words. As you speak kindness to yourself in front of the mirror, you are tending to the wounds that others may have inflicted, and you are reclaiming your power.

A Tool for Transformation: Building Resilience

Resilience is not just about bouncing back; it's about using adversity as a catalyst for growth. Mirror Talk becomes a tool for transformation as it encourages you to see your scars not as flaws, but as badges of honor. Those lines etched on your heart tell a story of survival, of overcoming challenges that tested your limits. Mirror Talk empowers you to embrace these stories and use them as stepping stones towards becoming the person you were always meant to be.

Cultivating a Positive Mindset: The Mirror as a Friend

Imagine the mirror as a dear friend, one who listens without judgment and offers unwavering support. Through Mirror Talk, you're not just speaking to yourself; you're cultivating a positive mindset and nurturing a friendship with the person you see in the mirror. Over time, this relationship blossoms into an unbreakable bond, one that encourages you to be kinder to yourself, to celebrate your victories, and to acknowledge your growth.

The Ripple Effect: Inspiring Others

Your journey of survival, self-discovery, and self-love has the power to inspire others who have faced similar trials. By sharing the practice of Mirror Talk, you can create a ripple effect of healing and empowerment. Imagine a world where survivors of domestic violence and divorce stand before their mirrors, speaking words of love and strength, reclaiming their identities, and rewriting their narratives.

In the tapestry of your life, faith is the thread that weaves through every triumph and trial, binding them together with purpose and meaning. Just as a mirror reflects your external image, let your faith reflect the divine spark within you – a reminder that you are a masterpiece created by the hands of a loving Creator. With each whispered affirmation, let faith be your guiding star, illuminating the path of self-discovery and illuminating the truth that you are fearfully and wonderfully designed. So, as you stand before the mirror, let faith infuse your words with power, reminding you that you are enough, you are strong, and you are destined for greatness. This chapter is just the beginning, a testament to the unyielding faith that will keep you returning to the mirror of self-discovery, ready to embrace the journey ahead with unwavering belief in yourself and the infinite possibilities that lie before you.

In the symphony of life, faith is the melody that resonates in your heart, guiding you through the highs and lows with a sense of purpose. Just as a mirror reflects your outer beauty, let your faith reflect the inner radiance that shines even brighter. With each word of affirmation spoken in front of the mirror, let faith be the anchor that grounds you, reminding you of your worthiness and the boundless potential that resides within. Just as faith has carried you through challenges before, let it be the driving force that compels you to return to the mirror time and time again. Embrace the transformative power of faith-infused Mirror Talk, and as you do, watch how your reflection becomes a testament to the journey of a woman of faith who stands strong, radiates love, and inspires others to embark on their own voyage of self-discovery.

In conclusion, the practice of Mirror Talk is a profound gift you can give to yourself. It's a practice that acknowledges the trials you've faced, the battles you've won, and the person you've become. As you gaze into the mirror, remember that the reflection looking back at you is not just a survivor; it's a warrior who has emerged from the fires of adversity, stronger and more beautiful than ever before. So, stand tall, speak kindly, and embrace the power of Mirror Talk – a practice that holds the key to unlocking the limitless potential that resides within you. In the sacred space of the mirror, you hold the key to your own transformation. The practice of Mirror Talk is a portal to self-discovery, a journey of healing, and a path towards unwavering self-love. As you continue to stand before that reflection, remember that you are not alone – you have the power to rewrite your story, to conquer the trials of life, and to inspire others to do the same. So, let your mirror become a sanctuary of empowerment, a canvas for the words that will shape your destiny. Just as faith moves mountains, let your mirror reflect the brilliance that keeps you coming back for more, guided by the unwavering faith that you are beautifully and wonderfully made.

In the chapters of your life, faith is the narrative that weaves through every page, offering solace in adversity and illuminating the beauty within. Just as a mirror reveals your external form, let your faith reveal the unshakeable spirit that resides in your soul. With each encouraging word spoken before the mirror, let faith be the steady rhythm that beats in your heart, reminding you of your inherent worth and the limitless possibilities ahead. Like a wellspring of inspiration, let faith draw you back to the mirror, where each reflection becomes a canvas for self-love and growth. The story of your life, interwoven with the fabric of faith, invites others to return eagerly for more, to witness the captivating journey of a woman whose mirror talk reflects not only her reflection but the enduring power of who she will continue to grow to be.

Examples of Mirror Talk: when coming out of adversity the residue of heartache and disappointment may still be present which is natural during your healing process. Remember you are still more than a conqueror and allow yourself to be honest about what your feelings as you heal. An example of mirror talk when feeling the residue of heartache would be.

This is my pain. It doesn't feel good but I'm STANDING in it. This, too, shall pass.

Example when feeling confused: I may not understand why this is happening (name what you're confused about) but, I am not confused about who I am. I am a child of God, and he cares for the matters of my heart therefore I will accept the peace he set aside just for me.

Example of Mirror talk when in doubt: Even though the circumstances around me are speaking doubt to my heart. I believe all things work together for my good, because I love the Lord and know that he guides my path.

Example when wrestling with self-confidence: I am fearfully and wonderfully made.

I am confident and capable!

I am a living proof of God's existence!

God has blessed me with strength before and he will do it again!

The words you speak to yourself hold Power!

Speak to yourself in your power with Mirror Talk!

ABOUT AUTHOR
Karlita Renata Green

Karlita Renata Green is a U.S. Army Veteran who served honorably for over 12 years, completing her military career July 14, 2014. Throughout Karlita's life she has always embodied an inner desire to serve and help others however she was able to. It was never her plan to join the Military but, it was God's plan and a way she chose to provide for her children. Karlita also became a licensed Cosmetologist and a Hair Replacement Specialist which led to her starting her first business called Exhilarating Hair studio where she assists female and male Veterans with medical hair loss to boost their self-confidence.

Karlita vowed that her challenging experiences would not define her nor validate her. Instead, she made the decision to overcome her circumstances and improve the direction of her life, the lives of her children and whomever God would send her way to encourage by stating her story and listening to others story. Karlita is realizing her dream to be a published author and Life Coach She is currently working on her memoir that will be entitled, "Unapologetically Free." She hopes that her story will be a blueprint and guide that will inspire others who may find themselves faced with difficult circumstances.

Karlita is also a co-author of a very inspirational and powerful book entitled "Champion Mindset" Her chapter within the book is "The Power of Perseverance" Karlita is from Demopolis, Alabama, raised in Colorado and Virginia due to being a military child.

Karlita recognizes that her purpose is to encourage others who have experienced life experiences similar to her own. She chooses to be a beacon of hope that others may need to know their past traumas do not have to define their future legacy. When she is not writing, Karlita enjoys reading, and spending time with family and friends. Her faith, strong will, and determination helped to redefine her future.

Connect with Karlita:

Authenticallykarlita@gmail.Com

FINAL THOUGHTS
By Dr. Pamela Henkel

As I sit here, penning the final words of this remarkable journey, I am enveloped in a surge of gratitude and astonishment. To see this dream crystallized on paper, to have navigated through each chapter alongside my community of authors—my cherished Jedi Scribes—is a sensation that words barely capture.

Each chapter reaffirms my belief that this is not just a book—it's a beacon, illuminating the path to self-betterment. It's the embodiment of countless hours, shared insights, and a collective spirit dedicated to the art of self-discovery. Jedi Scribes, your invaluable contributions have been the cornerstone of this journey with me. Thank you SO much ❤

Reading through these pages has been a surreal experience, akin to watching a dream unfold. My heart swells with pride and joy, knowing that what was once an abstract vision has now manifested into a tangible guide for so many.

To you, dear reader, if you're delving into this conclusion, I sincerely hope that these pages have equipped you with the insights, answers, and direction you've sought. May they act as the compass leading you towards embracing Your NEXT Best You.

Thank you for joining us on this transformative journey. Here's to every step you take in becoming Your NEXT Best version of You. 💙

In every moment lies the potential for growth. Seize it, embrace it, and let the journey to your next best self begin."
- Dr. Pamela Henkel

"Now faith brings our hopes into reality and becomes the foundation needed to acquire the things we long for. It is all the evidence required to prove what is still unseen."
Hebrews 11:1 TPT

BLESSINGS♥,

Straighten Your Crown 👑

Dr. Pamela Henkel